THE CRITICS DEBATE

General Editor: Michael Scott

The Critics Debate

General Editor: Michael Scott

PUBLISHED TITLES:

Sons and Lovers Geoffrey Harvey
Bleak House Jeremy Hawthorn
The Canterbury Tales Alcuin Blamires
Tess of the D'Urbervilles Terence Wright
Hamlet Michael Hattaway
The Waste Land / Ash Wednesday
   Arnold P. Hinchliffe
Othello Peter Davison
Paradise Lost Margarita Stocker
King Lear Ann Thompson
The Tempest David Daniell
Coriolanus Bruce King
Blake: Songs of Innocence and Experience
   David W. Lindsay
The Winter's Tale Bill Overton
Gulliver's Travels Brian Tippett
The Great Gatsby Stephen Matterson
To The Lighthouse Su Reid
Protrait of a Lady / Turn of the Screw
   David Kirby
Hard Times Allen Samuels
Philip Larkin Stephen Regan
Measure for Measure T. F. Wharton
Wuthering Heights Peter Miles
The Metaphysical Poets Donald Mackenzie
Heart of Darkness Robert Burden
Henry IV, Parts I and II Ronald Knowles

KING LEAR

Ann Thompson

MACMILLAN

First published 1988 by
THE MACMILLAN PRESS LTD
Houndmills, Basingstoke, Hampshire RG21 2XS
and London
Companies and representatives
throughout the world

ISBN 0–333–39585–9 hardcover
ISBN 0–333–39586–7 paperback

A catalogue record for this book is available
from the British Library.

Printed in Hong Kong

Reprinted 1993

Contents

General Editor's Preface	6
A Note on Text and References	7
Introduction	9
Part One: Survey	**11**
Formal, structural and generic approaches	11
Historical and social approaches	21
Religious and philosophical approaches	30
Approaches to staging and performance	42
Specialised approaches, key words, scenes and metaphors	51
Part Two: Appraisal – the Greatness of *King Lear*	**59**
The literary canon and the classic text	60
Challenging the evaluation of *King Lear*	67
Displacing the value argument	73
Afterword	81
References	82
Index	91

General Editor's Preface

OVER THE last few years the practice of literary criticism has become hotly debated. Methods developed earlier in the century and before have been attacked and the word 'crisis' has been drawn upon to describe the present condition of English Studies. That such a debate is taking place is a sign of the subject discipline's health. Some would hold that the situation necessitates a radical alternative approach which naturally implies a 'crisis situation'. Others would respond that to employ such terms is to precipitate or construct a false position. The debate continues but it is not the first. 'New Criticism' acquired its title because it attempted something fresh, calling into question certain practices of the past. Yet the practices it attacked were not entirely lost or negated by the new critics. One factor becomes clear: English Studies is a pluralistic discipline.

What are students coming to advanced work in English for the first time to make of all this debate and controversy? They are in danger of being overwhelmed by the cross-currents of critical approaches as they take up their study of literature. The purpose of this series is to help delineate various critical approaches to specific literary texts. Its authors are from a variety of critical schools and have approached their task in a flexible manner. Their aim is to help the reader come to terms with the variety of criticism and to introduce him or her to further reading on the subject and to a fuller evaluation of a particular text by illustrating the way it has been approached in a number of contexts. In the first part of the book a critical survey is given of some of the major ways the text has been appraised. This is done sometimes in a thematic manner, sometimes according to various 'schools' or 'approaches'. In the second part the authors provide their own appraisals of the text from their stated critical standpoint, allowing the reader the knowledge of their own particular approaches from which their views may in turn be evaluated. The series therein hopes to introduce and to elucidate criticism of authors and texts being studied and to encourage participation as the critics debate.

Michael Scott

A Note on Text and References

ALL quotations from *King Lear* are from the New Penguin Shakespeare text edited by G. K. Hunter (Harmondsworth, 1972). Other Shakespeare quotations are from *The Riverside Shakespeare*, edited by G. Blakemore Evans (Boston, Mass., 1974). The line references supplied (usually in *square* brackets, though sometimes in the main text) relate to these editions.

Critical works discussed are cited by author/editor and date of publication. References in the text appear in *round* brackets, and page references are given on their own where the source is unchanged. Details of the sources cited are listed in the References section at the end of the book.

For Kenneth Muir

Introduction

AN ENORMOUS work in every sense, *King Lear* has attracted an enormous quantity of critical writing: a recent bibliography lists 2500 items on the play published between 1940 and 1978 (Champion, 1980). Moreover, *King Lear* has always aroused critical controversy and debate. Questions such as 'Can it really be staged?', 'Is the death of Cordelia gratuitously shocking?' and 'Is Lear himself redeemed?' are only some of those which have been posed ever since it was first performed.

In recent times the output of critics has been rising sharply. Champion's bibliography shows that in the 1940s the average number of publications on *King Lear* per year was only 10. (This is the figure for 'criticism' alone, excluding publications on sources, dating, textual studies, bibliographies, editions, stage history, adaptations, influences and synopses.) In the 1950s the figure rose modestly to 16 per year, but in the 1960s it jumped dramatically to 45. Admittedly this average was boosted by a remarkable 90 publications in 1964, the quartercentenary of Shakespeare's birth, but even without that year the average would have risen to 30. In the 1970s it rose again to 54, and it seems very likely that the final figure for the 1980s will be higher still.

Obviously a book such as the present one cannot hope to provide complete coverage of all this critical activity without degenerating into a mere list of names and dates. I have had to be selective, and in Part One I have tried to pinpoint what seem to me the most important debates, both historically and currently. The grounds for controversy can and do shift over time. For example, most modern critics, unlike their predecessors, take it for granted that *King Lear* can in fact be staged. On the other hand, some contemporary approaches are challenging the traditional consensus of Christian and neo-Christian or humanist interpretations. Modern feminist critics are worried less by the fact of Cordelia's death than by what they see as Lear's appropriation of her – at the end of the play just as much as at the beginning.

The main emphasis in my survey of criticism in Part One is on twentieth-century writing and on the current debates about *King Lear*, but it has often seemed both necessary and helpful to look back into the past to explore the origins and developments of critical traditions. On the whole I have tried to present Part One as a relatively objective survey, not allowing my personal views to dominate, but of course the very choice of categories and arrangement of material is bound to privilege some critical approaches and under-represent others. It will be immediately apparent to the reader that many critics, both past and present, do not always fit neatly into the categories I have devised, and the same names will occur in two or more sections.

In Part Two I have decided to consider the phenomenon of 'The Greatness of *King Lear*'. Despite many doubts and misgivings expressed in the past and the sometimes heated debates about its merits, *King Lear* today is widely acclaimed as one of the greatest works in English literature. Without necessarily wishing to overturn or attack this position, it did seem important to investigate it. Beginning with a survey of the wider issues involved in the status of 'classic' texts and the formation and perpetuation of literary 'canons', I have also discussed some of the more interesting arguments put forward by critics who have questioned the high evaluation of *King Lear*, and the arguments of contemporary critics whose approaches have the effect of displacing traditional evaluations altogether. Finally, I have offered some speculations on the likely critical fortunes of the play in the immediate future.

Part One:
Survey

Formal, structural and generic approaches

What *kind* of literary text is *King Lear*? Where does the story come from? What shape or structure does it take? What genre or category of literary production does it fall into? The most obvious quick answer to these questions – that *King Lear* is a dramatic tragedy – leads immediately to further questions: What is tragedy? (A notoriously difficult one to answer.) And what indeed is drama? We are today, like the vast majority of critics of *King Lear* from the eighteenth century onwards, living in a society which no longer produces 'tragedy' as such, and we use the term 'drama' to cover everything from religious ritual to television soap opera. If we hastily add 'Jacobean' to our definition – *King Lear* is a Jacobean dramatic tragedy – we have acknowledged that it was produced in a very specific time and place but we have set ourselves the task of defining that historical context.

I shall discuss the very complex question of *King Lear* and history in the next section; here I want to survey approaches to the play which focus on its form, its structure and its genre. Critical debate has centred on three principle questions: Is the form in which we find the play in modern editions a fair representation of Shakespeare's final draft? What are the origins of the play's materials and how did Shakespeare shape, develop and combine them? Apart from 'tragedy', what other literary genres or categories might be relevant?

The text

It is daunting but necessary at the outset to have to contend with the fact that the most controversial issue in the critical

debate about *King Lear* today is over the question of the
authority of the text or texts. Before we can discuss the play
properly we need to know if what we have in front of us, in
the Penguin edition, the Arden edition, or any other edition,
is indeed 'the play' as Shakespeare intended it to be acted.
Since 1980 no fewer than four books have been published
(Stone, 1980; Urkowitz, 1980; Blayney, 1982; Taylor and
Warren, 1983) which challenge traditional assumptions about
the nature of the text and force every critic to reconsider this
fundamental issue.

There are two significant early texts of *King Lear*, the
Quarto (a small volume containing only the one play)
published in 1608, and the Folio (a large volume containing
nearly all of Shakespeare's plays) published in 1623. The
Quarto is a badly printed text, whereas the Folio was
produced with more care and contains fuller stage directions
as well as act and scene divisions. The Folio contains a
number of short passages amounting to more than 100 lines
of text which are not in the Quarto, but it omits some 300
lines of text which *are* in the Quarto. It is generally agreed
that the Folio text is based on the Quarto text altered by
reference to the promptbook actually used in performance:
this would account both for the greater care over stage
directions and for the cuts, which have hitherto been assumed
to be theatrical in origin: either the play was simply too long,
or some passages were thought not to have been effective on
stage. Almost all editions of *King Lear* currently available
conflate the two texts to produce the longest possible version of
the play.

Those who would challenge this editorial orthodoxy argue
that the two texts represent distinct stages in Shakespeare's
own development of *King Lear*: that the Quarto represents his
first version and that the Folio represents his own radical
revision, undertaken in order to improve the play on stage.
(This view is held by Urkowitz, Blayney, and Taylor and
Warren, but not by Stone.) Hence the traditional conflation
of the two texts is perceived as a muddle which was never
performed in Shakespeare's time and which fails to represent
either version clearly. The consequence of this line of argument
for the editor is to print not one but two separate texts of the
play, and the new Oxford edition is the first one to do that.

Once both texts become available in this way it will be possible for people other than textual scholars – students, teachers, critics and, perhaps even more importantly, actors and directors – to pursue the implications of such a radical development. It should be added that, while on the one hand not all textual scholars are convinced by the new theory, on the other hand very similar theories involving authorial revision are beginning to come forward in relation to *Hamlet* and *Othello*.

For many purposes, the new textual theory will not make an enormous amount of difference to critical accounts of the play. Very few of the pre-1980 critics whose work will be discussed in this book would have written very differently if they had held the new view of the text rather than the old one. The essential structure and meaning of the play remain the same in broad outlines in both texts. But we shall all have to be more careful, especially when we are discussing passages where the two texts differ, and we shall have to acknowledge that the alteration or omission or addition *may* be due to authorial revision rather than to theatrical exigency. Some specific implications of this are discussed below on pp. 56–7, and 75–6.

Sources and structure

By comparison with the heated debate that is currently in progress over the status of the text(s) of *King Lear*, there is a considerable degree of consensus about the actual sources of the play. It is universally agreed that the primary source for the story of King Lear and his daughters was the anonymous earlier play known as *The True Chronicle History of King Leir* (usually abbreviated to *King Leir* or just *Leir*), which was not published until 1605 but was probably performed in 1594 or earlier. Kenneth Muir has suggested in his Arden edition of *King Lear* (1952, p. xxix) that Shakespeare may even have acted in this play, taking the part of Perillus, the equivalent of Kent, who is on stage when a number of passages are spoken which are closely paralleled in Shakespeare's version. This account was supplemented by other versions of the Lear story in a range of contemporary sources, notably Raphael

Holinshed's *Chronicles*, Edmund Spenser's *The Faerie Queene* and John Higgins's *The Mirror for Magistrates*. Similarly, it is agreed that the sub-plot of *King Lear*, the story of Gloucester and his sons, derives from the story of the Paphlagonian King narrated by Sir Philip Sidney in his *Arcadia*. More general influences on the vocabulary, tone and thematic content of the play have been convincingly claimed for two other contemporary works, Montaigne's *Essays* (as translated by John Florio) and Samuel Harsnett's *A Declaration of Egregious Popish Impostures*.

So far, so good. Disagreement begins to arise, however, as soon as scholars and critics go beyond the mere identification of sources into the more speculative area of what Shakespeare did with those sources, how much he took from each of them, how and why he adapted and altered them, what kind of play he created by the accumulation and juxtaposition of his very heterogeneous materials. Everyone can agree that, in almost all the sources of her story known to Shakespeare, Cordelia commits suicide (the exception being the earlier *Leir* play, which ends happily with the reunion of Leir and Cordella, as she is called there), but, equally, everyone can put forward his or her own theory as to why precisely Shakespeare made this change and what it means for our interpretation of the play as a whole. In the same way it is a matter of record that Shakespeare drastically reduced the number of overtly Christian references that he found in *King Leir* (anyone can check this simply by counting), but, as we shall see in the 'Religious and philosophical approaches' section below, the extent to which his own *King Lear* is or is not a Christian play has been a major focus of debate.

Traditionally, source study has concerned itself primarily with *written* texts (and usually published ones, though some manuscripts have been admitted). The procedure is that, having noted a similarity between Shakespeare's play and some other text (play, poem, historical account, essay, sermon or whatever), one can establish a 'source' by investigating the order of composition of the two texts and hence the likelihood that Shakespeare did indeed 'borrow' if the other work is earlier. But this view of things may be altogether too narrow. The story of King Lear, like many of the other stories that Shakespeare used, was not invented by him or by any other named or nameless individual in Renaissance England; it can be seen rather as a timeless or archetypal narrative about the tensions of love and hatred within the family. It purports, in Shakespeare's version as well as in the earlier *Leir* play, to be some kind of 'chronicle history', but its historical material is of a legendary or mythical nature, quite unlike the more recent events of medieval history which Shakespeare had previously dramatised in the great sequence of English history plays he had written in the 1590s.

Consequently, some of the most interesting and controversial of recent work done on the 'matter' of *King Lear* has come from scholars who have ventured outside traditional literary studies into the terrain of myth, folklore and even psychoanalysis. We now know, thanks to the researches of folklorists, that behind the written sources of the Lear story is the oral folktale 'Love Like Salt', found in numerous versions all over the world (see Dundes, 1980). It can be argued that Shakespeare is deliberately exploring and exploiting the power of this primitive myth as he develops his basic themes of generation conflict and sibling rivalry (see Hoeniger, 1974). Some scholars have speculated in biographical terms about why Shakespeare, a man with two daughters of his own, was attracted to this particular subject; he did of course continue to explore father–daughter relationships in the late comedies, *Pericles, The Winter's Tale* and *The Tempest* (see Melchiori, 1960; and Barber, 1980). Furthermore, an acknowledgement of the darker implications of the folktale context – in particular the association of the 'Love Like Salt' story with tales of incest and adultery – may help us to understand the continuing power and fascination of the Lear story for subsequent generations of audiences and readers.

If the 'matter' of the play is, from this perspective, primitive, it is nevertheless true that Shakespeare's handling of it in terms of dramatic shape and structure is highly sophisticated. His decision to use a fully developed sub-plot, complicating the story of Lear and his daughters by adding to it the story of Gloucester and his sons, was unique amongst his tragedies and has been the subject of much debate. A. C. Bradley, whose work on *King Lear* has had an enormous influence on most of the critics mentioned in this book, found the double plot structure disadvantageous in terms of the potential confusion of characters and events and the consequent dissipation of interest for the audience or reader (1904; excerpted in Kermode, 1969, and Muir, 1984). This criticism, in one form or another, has frequently been repeated, perhaps most damagingly by those concerned with actually staging *King Lear* (see for example Webster, 1957).

Further, it has been objected that not only is the sub-plot confusing because of the sheer amount of material that it adds, but it is redundant in so far as it seems merely to repeat the main plot. Even such a critic as George Orwell, who vigorously defended the play against Tolstoy's famous attack (discussed in Part Two below), felt obliged to admit that this was a fault (Orwell, 1947; reprinted in Kermode, 1969, and Muir, 1984).

There have been two main lines of defence against this criticism. Several critics have chosen to emphasise the differences between the two plots rather than their similarities: a pre-Bradleyan critic, Richard Moulton (1885), compared Cordelia with Edmund rather than with her more obvious counterpart Edgar; Emrys Jones (1971) and others have emphasised the active role taken by Gloucester as he develops from being Edmund's dupe to taking his positive decision to assist the King – an activity which contrasts with Lear's increasing passivity and his status as victim in this part of the play. Bertrand Evans (1979) has discussed the elaborate structure of intrigue and disguise found in the sub-plot but not in the main plot, and I myself (Thompson, 1984) have written on the extent to which Shakespeare avoids some of the effects of repetition by his subtle manipulation of the ways in which parallels that are obvious to the audience are not perceived by the characters, and *vice versa*.

The more popular, indeed standard, justification of the sub-plot has however been to argue that it is a means of generalising and intensifying the main plot, thus making a virtue rather than an embarrassment of the degree of apparent repetition. It has been claimed that the effect is to give the play a universal or mythic quality (Empson, 1935), and that the sub-plot provides a series of careful mirrors and counterpoints throughout (Nevo, 1972).

At times, however, the defence has seemed a somewhat

equivocal one in so far as it has been implied that the sub-plot is intended as a cruder and more superficial version of the main plot. We are told, for example, that the sub-plot is 'in all respects less internalized and less serious than the main one' (Levin, 1971, p. 12). Does it really save the play from the charge of redundancy to argue that the sub-plot's chief value consists in its demonstrable inferiority? This would seem to be an equally serious criticism of Shakespeare's dramatic competence, and it has often had the unfortunate effect of producing dismissive and condescending readings of the sub-plot.

We are frequently assured that Lear's sufferings are more important because they are essentially spiritual, whereas poor Gloucester's are 'merely' physical; that Lear stands for the heroic quality of anger where Gloucester stands for lust (see for example Elton, 1966; excerpted in Kermode, 1969). In the face of this apparently coldhearted attitude, a number of critics have sprung to Gloucester's defence, admitting that his experiences parallel Lear's but arguing that they are equally or even more valuable. H. A. Mason, writing at about the same time as Emrys Jones, also found Gloucester the active focus of Act III and even considered him more worthy of our sympathy than Lear. His growth in self-knowledge is claimed to be greater and his experiences are generally seen as 'real' compared with the mixture of madness and play-acting surrounding Lear (Mason, 1970). A. L. French agreed with this assessment, supporting it by a comparison between Lear's 'prayer' expressing sympathy for the 'poor naked wretches' on the heath [III.iv.28–36] and Gloucester's speech on how 'distribution should undo excess' [IV.i.63–70], in which he finds the latter version superior in being more disinterested as well as more practical, since Gloucester actually begins by saying, 'Here, take this purse' (French, 1972).

Genre

While acknowledging that *King Lear* is primarily a tragedy, I have already suggested that it can be defined as a version of the chronicle history play or as a transformation of myth or folklore. These are by no means the only kinds or genres that have been invoked by critics in relation to this play. It should be emphasised at this point that, apart from a few neoclassical critics in the seventeenth and eighteenth centuries who were dubious about the propriety of mixing genres, all the critics discussed in this section are primarily involved in a *de*scriptive exercise, trying to understand certain aspects of the play through generic associations, rather than in a *pre*scriptive one, laying down rules and determining what ought or ought not to be done within each genre. The categories they employ are not meant to be either strictly defined or mutually exclusive.

Looking back into the annals of the English stage before Shakespeare, Oscar James Campbell (1948) has associated *King Lear* with the medieval morality play, a genre whose basic structure consists in the journey of a representative figure, usually called simply Mankind or Everyman, through a symbolic landscape of vices and virtues, temptations and rewards, towards death and salvation. The essentially Christian and optimistic implications of this generic parallel would be rejected by many critics, but Emrys Jones (1971) has emphasised the structural similarities, agreeing that the aim of the play, like that of its hero, is to 'crawl toward death' [i.i.41], a fact which accounts for the relatively inactive and unexciting mode of the play and for the number of scenes of a brooding, static nature. A modern version of this pattern has been suggested by Susan Snyder (1982), who finds in the play a number of parallels with the processes of death and dying as they are studied by twentieth-century psychologists and psychiatrists.

Drawing rather on the Jacobean theatrical context than on the medieval one, John Reibetanz (1977) has stressed the similarities between *King Lear* and a number of strictly contemporary plays by such writers as John Fletcher, George Chapman, Thomas Middleton and John Marston. He argues that some of the oddities of *Lear*, its improbabilities, its discontinuities, its violence, absurdity and moral simplicity, are all in fact characteristic of the Jacobean stage, and, moreover, that the very mixing of genres was itself normal at this time.

But by far the most popular generic labels critics have

attached to *King Lear* have been, perhaps surprisingly, those of comedy, tragicomedy, pastoral and romance. It has often been remarked that the play contains a large number of comic elements, including the double plot itself (unusual in tragedy of this period but very common in comedy), the presence of the professional Fool with his witty comments on the action, the central concern with the handing over of power from the older to the younger generation, the love affairs of the latter, the use of a natural setting (the heath) for educative purposes, the use of disguise, the flouting of probability in some aspects of the plotting. The play's principal sources, *King Leir* and the *Arcadia*, are themselves a comedy and a pastoral romance respectively, but critics have also located *King Lear* in the development of Shakespeare's own use of these genres.

Sometimes they look back to the period of the so-called festive comedies of the 1590s, observing in particular the number of parallels with *As You Like It*, another play in which we find interlocking groups of fathers and children, good and bad brothers, a plot in which families and lovers are sundered and some characters are obliged to sojourn in a 'wild place' (the Forest of Arden, compared with the heath) where identities are confused, changed and rediscovered, before the ultimate reunion and the return to court. If *King Lear* ended with the reunion of Lear and Cordelia in IV.vii it would reproduce this pattern quite closely, though the emphasis is on the older generation, the fathers rather than the children. (See especially Emrys Jones, 1971; Lindheim, 1974; and McCombie, 1980.)

Alternatively, critics have looked forward in Shakespeare's career to the late comedies or romances, in which the reunion of the family does indeed constitute the happy ending: the pattern is most obviously present in *Pericles* and *The Winter's Tale* but can also be seen in *Cymbeline* and *The Tempest*. In this respect *King Lear* becomes a sort of prologue to the later group as well as a recapitulation of the earlier group. John Danby (1952), Philip Edwards (1968) and Glynne Wickham (1973) have all written of it in this way.

But, as everyone admits, one of the most striking things about *King Lear* is that it does not end with the happy reunion but goes on to confront us with the deaths of both father and daughter. In so far as it incorporates the structures and devices of comedy, pastoral and romance, it seems to do so in order to negate or pervert them, almost sadistically holding out the hopes of harmony, reunion, self-discovery and a happy ending only to deny them with the overwhelming realities of pain, incomprehension and death.

Each one of its comic elements serves to increase the harshness of the tragedy. Discussing the sub-plot, often seen in comedy as a device for providing variety and a sense of space or largeness, Susan Snyder (1979) remarks that 'by introducing a potential contrast and then dissolving it in dreadful parallelism, Shakespeare converts the double plot from its usual freeing function to the service of tragic claustrophobia' (p. 141). The Fool does not so much provide comic relief as twist the knife in the wound and underline the fundamental horror of the play's events; Kent's disguise does not free him to become a new self but merely allows him to continue in his old role (and he is denied the pleasure of proper recognition), while Edgar's seems to have the negative effect of being the last straw which drives Lear mad.

The love affairs between Edmund, Goneril and Regan are the opposite of innocent romance, and the play's overtly comic scenes, usually involving the Fool and Kent, 'do not relieve but rather heighten the tragic movement' (Orgel, 1980). As for the sojourn in the 'wild place', Maynard Mack has called *King Lear* 'the greatest anti-pastoral ever penned' (1965), David Young terms it 'pastoral turned inside out' (1972), and Ronald Miller describes it as 'the photographic negative of a pastoral comedy' (1975). All three consider the play's use of pastoral to be ironic, emphasising the cruelty and the alien side of nature, not its comforting or healing powers. Michael Long (1976) is, however, slightly more hopeful: having said that the *shape* of festive comedy is present in *Lear* without the *tone*, he does not find the use of pastoral elements to be entirely negative but insists on the complexity of the final effect – the rejuvenation of society, though painful and violent, has in some measure been achieved despite the appalling cost. Certainly it can be said that the deaths in v.iii would be even more intolerable without the reunion in iv.vii, even if that happiness is so quickly destroyed.

One particularly influential generic approach has stressed the grotesqueness or absurdity of the play's comic effects. The ghoulish horrors of the Jacobean stage often seem to hover on the edge of the ludicrous, but G. Wilson Knight (1930; excerpted in Kermode, 1969, and Muir, 1984) found a grotesque comedy throughout *King Lear*, beginning in the opening scene, in which Lear's anger is foolish and pathetic – absurd as well as frightening. The Fool's role, Knight says, reminds us of 'the humour of cruelty and the cruelty of humour' (p. 124 in Kermode), and the scenes on the heath are mad, fantastical and sinister in an almost hysterical way: 'In no tragedy of Shakespeare does incident and dialogue so recklessly and miraculously walk the tightrope of our pity over the depths of bathos and absurdity' (p. 127). The climax comes in iv.vi with the bathos of Gloucester's failure to commit suicide and the grotesque and ludicrous encounter between Lear and Gloucester.

While brilliantly pointing up the absurd comedy of the play, Knight's reading was not a totally negative one. Although the suffering of Lear and Gloucester is intensified by the grotesque treatment, it is not in the end meaningless. But, when Jan Kott revived and updated Knight's approach by writing of *King Lear* as a play akin to Beckett's *Endgame* (Kott, 1965; excerpted in Kermode, 1969), this positive side had vanished. For Kott, *Lear*, like the Absurd drama of Ionesco and Dürrenmatt as well as Beckett, depicts a world in which existence itself is absurd or grotesque rather than tragic. Gloucester's suicide attempt is no more than a theatrical trick, a pantomime on an empty stage: there are no longer any gods, so such a gesture can have no meaning. It is appropriate, in this reading, that the King himself takes over the clown's role after the Fool disappears.

Historical and social approaches

The events of *King · Lear* ostensibly take place in a remote period of British history, though the Fool is allowed to joke about this when he announces 'This prophecy Merlin shall make; for I live before his time' [iii.ii.95–6]. On the other hand, a number of references in the play seem to imply a very different sort of context: people talk about bourgeois professionals such as lawyers, surgeons, apothecaries, moneylenders, monopoly-holders, politicians and schoolmasters. The characters are clearly not dressed in primitive furs or rags, since they refer to breeches, worsted stockings, gloves, buttons, cod-pieces and spectacles. As we shall see in the section on 'Approaches to staging and performance', attempts to give the play a consistently primitive setting have proved problematic, though at the same time it is clear that Shakespeare made some specific efforts to distinguish the manners, beliefs and social institutions of his characters from those of himself and his audience.

That audience would not have been particularly surprised to see legendary British history dramatised on the contemporary stage. Apart from the earlier *Leir* play itself, a number of previous plays, including *Gorboduc, Locrine, The Birth of Merlin* and *The Misfortunes of Arthur*, had been set in a comparably vague and internally inconsistent Ancient Britain. The more serious plays of this type had used their material in the same way as the Elizabethans customarily used more recent historical material – as a body of narratives that could be drawn upon for didactic purposes. They purported to teach political lessons and to provide graphic examples of how monarchs and their subjects ought (or more often ought not) to behave. This was one obvious way of making ancient history relevant to the audience, but critics have argued that *King Lear* is specifically 'Jacobean' in a number of other ways as well.

The topical and the prophetic

In the most immediate sense, it has been claimed that the Lear story would have had a topical relevance in the early seventeenth century because of the parallel case of one Brian Annesley, an old servant of Queen Elizabeth, whose daughter Grace attempted in October 1603 to have him declared lunatic and unfit to govern his affairs. His youngest daughter Cordell defended him and succeeded in inheriting his property when he died in 1604, although her sister contested the will.

Geoffrey Bullough prints some documents relating to this case, which was going on at about the time *King Lear* was being written, in his *Narrative and Dramatic Sources of Shakespeare* (vii, 1973), and C. J. Sisson (1962) has found two other contemporary cases of a similar nature.

Paradoxically, it can also be claimed that Shakespeare's very choice of the particular and apparently remote narrative of King Lear can itself be seen as evidence of his sensitivity to topical issues in another sense. The Lear story is part of the much larger narrative of legendary British history that begins with Brutus escaping from the fall of Troy and establishing his kingdom in Britain. On his death he divided the kingdom between his three sons with disastrous results (dramatised in *Locrine*). This fatal division, though this time between two sons, was repeated by Gorboduc (dramatised in the play of that name), and all three stories of division (that is, including the Lear one) were linked with Merlin's prophecy of the coming of a second Brutus who would rule in New Troy (a name actually used for London in a number of pageants and civic celebrations in Elizabethan and Jacobean times) and reunite the kingdom. As Glynne Wickham (1973) points out, this figure had already been recognised in the person of James I (who had of course united Scotland and England) by such writers as Samuel Daniel, Thomas Dekker and Anthony Munday, so it could be argued that Shakespeare also associated the Lear story with the accession of James I.

The material is, then, both historical and prophetic. The prophecies from the past can be interpreted as looking forward to the Jacobean present, but, more explicitly, the play also contains references which look forward to the end of the world. When the blind Gloucester meets the mad Lear, he comments, 'O ruined piece of nature! This great world/Shall so wear out to naught' [iv.vi.135–6], and later Kent and Edgar ask, 'Is this the promised end?/Or image of that horror?' [v.iii.261–2]. The play's obsession with Doomsday and Apocalypse, noted by Holloway (1961; excerpted in Kermode, 1969), Mack (1965) and Lascelles (1973), has been explored in great detail in a recent book by Joseph Wittreich (1984), who argues that this interest was very widespread at the time, arising partly out of the association of both Queen Elizabeth and James I with apocalyptic myths. Its presence in the play is complex: on the one hand it adds to the enormity and solemnity of the actual tragic conclusion, but on the other hand its wider implications are more optimistic: the catastrophic divisions of the world within the play must be read as a *reverse* image of the union and harmony of the Jacobean court where *King Lear* was presented (as a Boxing Day entertainment!) in 1606. Moreover, even within the play-world, some important characters survive the catastrophe – notably Edgar, whose name, according to F. T. Flahiff (1974), makes him also a 'once and future king', associating him as it does with the good Saxon King Edgar, who rid England of wolves. In Edgar's triumph over Edmund and his prospective rule of the kingdom the bleakness of the ending is partially alleviated.

Medieval and modern

King Lear is inevitably influenced by the philosophical, religious, political and social ideas of its time in many other ways too. In the section on 'Religious and philosophical approaches' I shall be discussing the work of such scholars as William R. Elton (1966) and Paul A. Jorgensen (1967), who have, respectively, researched the background of Jacobean thinking on religion and on self-discovery and related their findings to the play. But it would be wrong to suppose that the play 'reflects' its time in a simple or straightforward way. Historical reality is always very complex and usually contradictory. Many changes were taking place in England in the early seventeenth century and no consensus can be assumed. It is indeed one of the marks of the greatness of *King Lear* for L. C. Knights (1959) that, besides being 'timeless and universal' and having 'a crucial place in its author's inner biography', it 'marks a moment of great importance in the changing consciousness of the civilisation to which it belongs' (p. 84). He analyses this changing consciousness in terms of attitudes towards the concept of Nature, drawing on the work of John F. Danby (1949).

Everyone would agree that 'Nature' is an important concept in *King Lear*, frequently referred to and significantly introduced in the two opening scenes with Lear's rejection of

Cordelia as 'a wretch whom Nature is ashamed/Almost t'acknowledge hers' [I.i.212–13] and Edmund's speech beginning 'Thou, Nature, art my goddess' [I.ii.1]. The play could almost be seen as a sustained punning meditation on the fact that Edmund, being illegitimate, is what we rather oddly call the 'natural' son of Gloucester. When the characters, as they often do, define behaviour as 'natural' or 'unnatural', they are evoking a whole set of unstated assumptions about the 'proper' relations that should prevail in society between king and subject, father and child, master and servant, man and woman.

Shakespeare's position in relation to these proprieties has been debated, as we shall see, but in 1949 Danby distinguished between two different attitudes to Nature in *King Lear*, the old traditional one and the new revolutionary one. In the old view, Nature is seen in a positive way as generous and benign, expressing itself through social order and harmony. In the newer, more modern view, it is seen in a negative way as merely indifferent, something to be manipulated. The shift is from an essentially religious view of the world and the place of men and women in it to an agnostic one, and Danby exemplifies this shift in thinking from the philosophical writings of Bacon and Hooker to those of Hobbes, whose cynical, materialistic, competitive world view would eventually replace the more comforting one inherited from the Middle Ages. Not surprisingly, the good characters in the play – the King himself, Cordelia, Gloucester, Kent and Edgar – are associated by Danby with the old view of Nature, whereas the bad characters – Edmund, Goneril, Regan and Cornwall – are associated with the new view. In the most extreme reading, Cordelia embodies beneficent Nature while Edmund represents the Hobbesian New Man.

This shift from medieval to modern has been argued in social and economic readings of *King Lear* as well as in religious and philosophical ones. Marshall McLuhan claimed that '*King Lear* is a kind of elaborate case history of people translating themselves out of a world of roles into the new world of jobs' and that the play 'offers a complete demonstration of how it felt to live through the change from medieval to Renaissance time and space' (1962, p. 14). This approach has informed a number of recent essays with titles

such as 'Reason and Need: *King Lear* and the Crisis of the
Aristocracy' (Colie, 1974a), '*King Lear* and the Decline of
Feudalism' (Delany, 1977) and 'The Breakdown of Medieval
Hierarchy in *King Lear*' (Serpieri, 1979). Thus it is claimed
that the ancient story of King Lear is used by Shakespeare to
investigate and comment on the much more recent story of
the transition of British society from feudalism to capitalism.
This is not as unlikely as it might seem at first sight: many of
the play's crises and points of conflict can be related very
directly to Jacobean experience. Rosalie L. Colie, who reads
King Lear in the light of the historian Lawrence Stone's *The
Crisis of the Aristocracy, 1558–1641* (1965), finds it to be 'a play
deeply rooted in its own period, a play which draws some of
its power from the playwright's insight into the peculiar
aristocratic situation of the time in which it was written'
(Colie, 1974a, p. 189). Remarking on the apparently
deliberate vagueness and allusiveness of the text, she is yet
able to point to 'moments of exact social observation and
commentary' (p. 191).

King Lear's central concern with the problems of property
and inheritance can certainly be seen as topical. The issue of
royal inheritance in particular was a subject of anxious
debate at a time when several European royal families had
died out or seemed on the verge of doing so. Lear's solution
to the problem of lacking a male heir, the division of the
kingdom between his daughters, turns out disastrously, but
Gloucester's more orthodox reliance on primogeniture does
not save him. Lear's daughters can disregard him once they
have taken away his retinue, a crucial source of support not
just psychologically but in practical terms for a monarch
trying to hold power without a professional army in a society
where large landowners customarily maintained threatening
bands of armed servants. According to Lawrence Stone, the
enormous expansion of the gentry and the commercial classes
in comparison to the nobility during the period from 1558 to
1641 led to something of an identity crisis for the older
aristocracy, who were keen to distinguish themselves from
the newly rich. The snobbery of birth and class against
money is apparent in a large number of Jacobean plays (for
example, in the 'city comedies'), and seems in *King Lear* to lie
behind the extraordinary venom with which the aristocratic

Kent, despite the fact that he is pretending to be the lower-class Caius, attacks Oswald as 'a base, proud, shallow, beggarly, three-suited, hundred-pound, filthy-worsted-stocking knave' and so on [ii.ii.13–15].

The English aristocracy did of course have good reason to be worried about a general decline in paternal authority in the early seventeenth century. The loosening of the old feudal and hierarchical ties of medieval paternalism was after all going to lead to a civil war during the lifetime of some of the younger members of the audience for *King Lear*, and in that war the aristocracy would itself be divided and its automatic assumption of authority would be violently challenged by the deposition and beheading of the King. When *King Lear* was rewritten by Nahum Tate during the Restoration (in 1681), it is significant that the happy ending he provided for it gave the audience the double image of the king as martyr and the king restored. King James II, like everyone else at the time, preferred this version; he saw it twice – not that this prevented him from becoming another martyr king himself.

The attitudes towards money that we find in *King Lear* are particularly interesting in the light of its topical economic context. As Colie says, the actual economics of the play are vague and the monetary units referred to (pounds, shillings, pence and so on) are, like so many other details, anachronistic, but nevertheless 'it is difficult not to read from this play a profound critique of habits of quantification induced by a commercial revolution' (Colie, 1974a, p. 190). Again it is a case of the old world *versus* the new. In this area, the old ethos is (in its idealised picture of itself) one of unreckoned generosity, magnificence and carelessness, whereas the new values stress providence, frugality, even calculation. Lear and Cordelia talk the language of free giving, while Goneril, Regan and Edmund think quantitatively, they put a price on things, they ask coldly, 'What need one?' [ii.iv.258]. Of course, the older generation is not blameless in this respect. Lear begins the play with the foolish and fatal game of making his daughters 'pay' for their shares of the kingdom with inflated declarations of love, and he and Gloucester both turn, slowly and painfully, from their own unhappy experiences of the distribution of their personal property to a more general perception of the concept of necessity and the

harsh realities of poverty from which their social positions
had hitherto shielded them.

The text and the world

But again it is important to remember that *King Lear* cannot
be 'explained' in terms of a historical thesis, any more than it
can be used to 'prove' or illustrate that thesis. L. C. Knights
was worried some time ago by historical interpretations of
Shakespeare's plays which seemed to him too narrow and
over-schematic (1955), and Francis Schoff has expressed
similar doubts about reducing Shakespeare to 'a mere puppet
of the Zeitgeist' (1962). Any assumption that historical
scholarship is able to provide especially authoritative readings
is by now, in any case, challenged by the number of different
interpretations of the history of the period on offer.

For a long time after its first publication, E. M. W.
Tillyard's *The Elizabethan World Picture* (1943) dominated this
field, giving literary critics their main notions of the political
and ideological background to Shakespeare's plays. Tillyard's
'picture' is of an orderly hierarchical world whose elaborate
systems of correspondence and interdependence were
ultimately guaranteed by divine authority. Shakespeare could
hardly help being part of this world, but Tillyard argued
further that, without being very consciously 'political', he
strongly endorsed its essentially conservative values. Critics
such as Danby, reading *King Lear* in the light of these
assumptions, find in the play a nostalgia for the old orderly
past and a revulsion towards the present; Shakespeare aligns
himself with the aristocracy against the self-made men – an
inconsistent but not unfamiliar attitude for a man who was
himself self-made. (See also Kernan, 1981.)

But Tillyard's picture has been challenged, both by those
who say it over-simplifies history and by those who say it
over-simplifies Shakespeare. Modern historians such as
Lawrence Stone demonstrate that the period was not one
of cosy ideological harmony but was full of anomalies,
inconsistencies and tensions. Colie's use of his book brings a
significant new emphasis to the analysis of the Lear world
and raises many more doubts about the meaning of the text:

she concludes that 'The moral weight of the play comes down decisively with the advocates of old values, but not without having hesitated long enough to show how crucially those values fell short' (1974a, p. 216). Stone's later book *The Family, Sex and Marriage in England, 1500–1800* (1977) has had a very strong influence on literary scholars, and there is by now an increasing number of people working on the borderlines of literary criticism and history. These scholars are sometimes termed the 'new historicists', and key recent works include Stephen Greenblatt's *Renaissance Self-Fashioning: From More to Shakespeare* (1980) and Jonathan Goldberg's *James I and the Politics of Literature* (1983). (I shall have more to say about this in Part Two.)

Much of the anti-Tillyard debate has centred on the history plays, but two recent discussions of *King Lear* have raised similar issues. Jonathan Dollimore, in his brief section on the play in *Radical Tragedy* (1984), argues for a 'materialist' reading of *King Lear* which emphasises its concern with power, property and inheritance. He insists that human values are 'not antecedent to material realities but are, on the contrary, in-formed by them' (p. 197). In so far as Edmund represents a focus of opposition to the older generation, his sceptical independence does not liberate him from their values. He can laugh at Gloucester's belief in astrological influences and deny the myth of his own innate inferiority, but he is still trapped within the dominant ideology of property and power. In fact, for Dollimore, *King Lear* demonstrates that there is no such thing as autonomous value: values are never absolute and abstract but are always dependent on political and social realities.

Stephen Greenblatt also attacks the notion of autonomy – in this case the supposed autonomy of the text itself – in 'Shakespeare and the Exorcists' (1985), a new historicist version of source-study which re-examines the relationship between *King Lear* and Samuel Harsnett's *A Declaration of Egregious Popish Impostures*. The 'impostures' with which Harsnett is concerned are exorcisms of evil spirits performed by priests. Harsnett is specifically attacking Jesuit exorcisms, but he had earlier written against a Puritan exorcist: he is not claiming a monopoly on the practice for the Anglican Church but rather exposing exorcism itself as a fraud. It has long been known that Shakespeare 'borrowed' from Harsnett the names of the foul fiends by whom Edgar, in his disguise as Poor Tom, claims to be possessed, along with some of his mad language, especially his allusions to hell. But what does this knowledge mean? Greenblatt rejects the model of *King Lear* as a free-standing work by a solitary genius, drawing almost accidentally on a range of 'raw materials' or 'backgrounds', and proposes instead a much more complex exploration of the institutions in which both *King Lear* and Harsnett's *Declaration* are embedded.

This involves an investigation of the role of the theatre in Jacobean society: Harsnett exposes the exorcisms as frauds by claiming that they are theatrical fictions, in effect plays put on by a few professionals (the Jesuits) who cunningly teach the 'possessed' how to play the roles assigned to them by a process of suggestion, the asking of leading questions and so on. Of course, Edgar's 'possession' in *King Lear* is equally fictitious (both at the level of the character and at that of the actor) but it is openly and explicitly so. At a deeper level, however, Greenblatt claims that Shakespeare's theatre is engaged in appropriating and secularising religious rituals and in the process emptying them of their old significance. The use of Harsnett in *King Lear* is topical not only in that it draws on a recent and sensational item of 'news', but also in a larger sense as indicative of an ongoing redefinition of values in which questions such as 'What is the sacred?' and 'How can society distinguish between legitimate and illegitimate claims to sacred authority?' were very much on the agenda. (See also Murphy, 1984.)

Religious and philosophical approaches

In what sense, if any, is *King Lear* a religious play? This has been one of the most hotly debated issues in *Lear* criticism, with extreme positions adopted both by those who read it as a Christian allegory of salvation and by those who read it as a grotesque parody which mocks and denies the possibility of any religious meaning. Of the earlier critics, Samuel Johnson was famously shocked by the ending, particularly by the death of Cordelia, which he found immoral and unjust (1765;

excerpted in Kermode, 1969, and Muir, 1984). A. C. Bradley, on the other hand, went so far as to suggest that an alternative title for the play might be 'The Redemption of King Lear', arguing that the business of 'the gods' with Lear was 'neither to torment him, nor to teach him a "noble anger", but to lead him to attain through apparently hopeless failure the very end and aim of life' (1904; excerpted in Kermode, 1969, and Muir, 1984; pp. 97–8 in Kermode).

Bradley's view was so popular that by 1960 Barbara Everett could claim that the 'orthodox' approach to the play was one which stressed its Christian content and almost overlooked the tragic ending in a determination to celebrate the positive aspects of suffering and patience, the triumph of reconciliation and love (1960; reprinted in Kermode, 1969). Her attack on this orthodoxy aroused a flurry of protests, including some indignant denials from those whom she had 'stigmatised' as Christian interpreters, but twelve years later it was still possible for A. L. French to claim that the 'received reading' of King Lear was the 'redemptive' one and to feel isolated and embattled in his rejection of it (1972). He was not in fact alone by then, as is apparent from G. R. Hibbard's survey of Lear criticism from 1939 to 1979 (1980). Hibbard identifies a crucial shift taking place around 1960 'not only in the controversy as to whether King Lear is, or is not a Christian tragedy, but also in critical assumptions and methods' (p. 9).

As Hibbard sees it, the shift is one away from 'ideological considerations' towards a greater emphasis on 'the poignantly human experience that King Lear embodies' (p. 10). In readings of this kind, human dignity is asserted by the courage and integrity of the individual: Lear's sufferings are justified not because they will earn him a place in a Christian heaven but because his endurance is heroic in itself. Likewise, Cordelia's virtue has to be its own reward: the fact that she not only 'loses' in this world but has no confident expectation of being compensated in the next serves if anything to heighten the heroism of her choices.

Most recently, critics have rejected this 'humanist' view as well as the Christian one. Dollimore, in the book previously cited (1984), argues that they are in fact alike in their preoccupation with 'essentialist subjectivity' – the free-standing individual consciousness whose experiences are ultimately affirmed or denied by the presence or absence of a theological framework. Instead, his materialist reading decentres individuals in order to make visible 'social process and its forms of ideological misrecognition' (p. 191). If Christian readings mystify (and justify) suffering as the basis of divine redemption, humanist readings likewise mystify it as the basis of *self*-redemption. Both remove it from the realm of social and historical reality. (Some of the consequences of this rejection of both Christian and humanist readings will be discussed in Part Two below.)

How are such radical disagreements possible? What kinds of evidence are being used? I shall try in the following pages to sketch the main outlines of what has been a very complex and long-sustained debate involving such large issues as the definition of tragedy itself and the decline of religious belief.

Pagan or Christian?

King Lear is supposedly set in a pre-Christian era. Characters refer to 'the gods' and to specific pagan deities – Jove, Juno, Apollo – rather than to Jesus Christ. On the other hand there is no doubt that its author was a Christian, perhaps formerly a Catholic (see Honigmann, 1985), and that his society, like ours, was thoroughly imbued with Christian concepts, values and assumptions. Some of these get into the play at a relatively trivial level, as for example when Kent claims to 'eat no fish' [i.iv.16], apparently alluding to the Christian practice of fasting, or when the Fool mentions 'holy-water' [iii.ii.10]. Others seem more significant: much has been made of the 'saintly' character of Cordelia, enhanced by the language of an anonymous Gentleman who describes her sorrow at hearing how her father has been treated in decidedly religious terms: 'she shook/The holy water from her heavenly eyes' [iv.iii.29–30], and by that of another Gentleman three scenes later who remarks, just after Lear has departed, 'Thou hast one daughter/Who redeems nature from the general curse/Which twain have brought her to' [iv.vi.205–7]. Thoroughgoing allegorists would identify the 'twain' (Goneril and Regan) with Adam and Eve, whose fall can only be redeemed by Christ (Cordelia).

Shakespeare's plays are notoriously full of inconsistencies and anachronisms at the level of incidental detail (clocks chime in ancient Rome, Cleopatra wears stays, King John's army is equipped with cannons, Hector is familiar with the works of Aristotle), but he did clearly go to some trouble to distinguish between his own society and pagan societies in crucial matters such as attitudes to death and the afterlife. Suicide is an important touchstone. In the Roman plays it is a heroic act which brings honour and admiration: 'Let's do't after the high Roman fashion', says Cleopatra, 'And make death proud to take us' [*Antony and Cleopatra*, iv.xv.87–8]. But Renaissance Christianity saw suicide as sinful and it is this attitude which is dominant in *King Lear*, where Edgar goes to some trouble to prevent Gloucester from killing himself, explaining to the audience, 'Why I do trifle thus with his despair / Is done to cure it' [iv.vi.33–4]. It is true that friends and servants are reluctant to help Brutus and Antony to kill themselves, but they are motivated by love, not by moral disapproval: Strato's eventual assistance of Brutus is seen by others as an honourable service, while Antony's servant Eros chooses to kill himself first and is acclaimed by Antony for his nobility. In this respect, *King Lear* is closer to Shakespeare's more ostensibly Christian plays such as *Hamlet*, in which the hero would be tempted to commit suicide if 'the Everlasting had not fix'd / His canon 'gainst self-slaughter' [i.ii.131–2], and there is some debate about whether Ophelia deserves to be 'buried in Christian burial when she wilfully seeks her own salvation' [v.i.1–2]. Hamlet deters Horatio from killing himself at the end, and the prevailing ethic would disapprove of such an action, just as in *Othello* the bystanders disapprove of Othello's suicide: 'All that is spoke is marr'd' [v.ii.356].

As for the afterlife, it is clear that the characters in *King Lear* do not suppose that death is simply annihilation, but rather assume the existence of some kind of heaven or hell where they will be rewarded or punished. Most obviously, Lear thinks he is already in the afterworld when he wakes in Cordelia's presence saying,

You do me wrong to take me out o'the grave.
Thou art a soul in bliss; but I am bound
Upon a wheel of fire, that mine own tears
Do scald like molten lead.

[IV.vii.45–8]

The 'wheel of fire' could be a classical allusion, but editors point out that it is also found in medieval Christian accounts of hell (see Muir, Arden edn., 1952, p. 178), and again Lear's attitude here is very comparable to that of the Christian Othello, who imagines Desdemona in heaven while he is in hell [*Othello*, v.ii.272–80]. At the end of *King Lear*, Kent responds to Albany's invitation to share in ruling the kingdom by telling him, 'I have a journey, sir, shortly to go./My master calls me, I must not say no' [v.iii.319–20]. The assumption is that he will follow Lear into the next world, and again the attitude is comparable to that of a more explicitly Christian retainer, the Bastard in *King John*, who responds to the death of his monarch by saying,

Art thou gone so? I do but stay behind
To do the office for thee of revenge,
And then my soul shall wait on thee to heaven,
As it on earth hath been thy servant still.

[v.iii.70–3]

Yet in *King Lear* the Christian attitudes are implicit rather than explicit in the text, a fact which becomes more obvious when we compare Shakespeare's play with its sources. It may use the morality pattern (see Campbell, 1948, and Emrys Jones, 1971), but there is no overt doctrinal message. Several critics have pointed out that the earlier *King Leir* play is saturated with specifically Christian piety – perhaps of a Puritanical cast (see James H. Jones, 1970–1) – and that Shakespeare must have acted deliberately in removing most of this frame of reference. At the same time, and almost inevitably, he incorporated numerous echoes from the Bible (see Colie, 1974b), and, as already discussed, he made use of Harsnett's attack on exorcism, which was a specifically Christian practice, though one which Harsnett and others wanted to abolish.

The most extensive study of the religious climate of *King Lear* in relation to contemporary Renaissance thinking is William R. Elton's *'King Lear' and the Gods* (1966). He explores the range of attitudes to concepts such as providence, atheism, paganism and superstition not only in the play's sources but in a wide range of other works from the period, and concludes that Shakespeare intended a relatively realistic depiction of a pagan society. Identifying four main attitudes that were ascribed to pagans in Jacobean times, he finds them displayed in the play's major characters: Cordelia and Edgar represent enlightened paganism; Goneril, Regan and Edmund represent pagan atheism; Gloucester represents pagan superstition; and Lear represents pagan agnosticism. Lear's progress through the play is that of a pagan who comes to doubt his gods. While finding overtly Christian or 'redemptive' readings of the play anachronistic or erroneous, Elton argues that the play's Christian references would have made the audience aware of a number of analogies between the pagan world of the play and their own Christian world with its theological debates and crises.

An opposite set of conclusions is, however, reached by Roy W. Battenhouse (1969), who employs an equally formidable degree of scholarship to argue that Shakespeare's Christian audience would most likely have read the play as a Christian parable. On the whole Elton's view, while striking many critics as over-schematic, has proved more influential, and his conclusion that the play is intended to depict a pagan world is confirmed by Robert G. Hunter (1976), who compares it with some indisputably Christian plays (*Richard III, Hamlet, Othello* and *Macbeth*) and agrees that it is a study of pagan agnosticism.

Suffering and redemption

There is of course no doubt that most of the virtuous characters in *King Lear* – Cordelia, Edgar and Kent, but most spectacularly Lear and Gloucester – undergo some kind of suffering, but critics have disagreed considerably about the meaning and value of those experiences. How far do the characters 'deserve' to suffer? Do their sufferings constitute

some kind of compensation for their crimes, whether of
commission or omission? Is the suffering in itself some kind
of index of virtue? Does it lead to moral redemption in a
religious sense, or to a greater degree of knowledge of the
self, of others, or of the world in general? Is there a god who
permits suffering, a god who uses suffering in a positive way
as some kind of test of human worth, a god who sadistically
delights in suffering, or no god at all?

The sheer intensity of the suffering in *King Lear*, relentlessly
enhanced by the many metaphors of the human body being
hurt or tortured, has generally been considered shocking, but
critics have responded to the shock in different ways. The
most crudely moralistic response – that the suffering is
justified because the characters need to be punished – is
stated by Edgar within the play when he speaks to his dying
brother of their father:

> The gods are just, and of our pleasant vices
> Make instruments to plague us:
> The dark and vicious place where thee he got
> Cost him his eyes.
>
> [v.iii.168–71]

Edmund accepts this harsh judgement on Gloucester, and a
number of critics have followed in his wake: Maynard Mack
assumes we are looking forward to Gloucester's exemplary
punishment from his very first appearance (Mack, 1965;
excerpted in Muir, 1984, pp. 232–3), though he has been
taken to task for this by William Empson (1967). Some
critics (Morris, 1957; Fleissner, 1962) even argue that
Cordelia deserves her fate, and contrive to find the whole
narrative morally uplifting.

More worthy of serious attention is the school of thought
which proposes that, regardless of whether the characters
deserve to suffer, their experiences can be seen in a positive
light in so far as they lead to some kind of improvement.
Bradley generously assumed that for Lear himself this is a
return to his real self: 'There is nothing more noble and
beautiful in literature than Shakespeare's exposition of the
effects of suffering in reviving the greatness and eliciting the
sweetness of Lear's nature' (1904; excerpted in Kermode,

1969, p. 97). This benign view has been elaborated in more or less religious terms by a large number of critics. G. Wilson Knight argued that the religion which emerges in *King Lear* is analogous to that of the Old Testament book of Job: the suffering is purifying and in some sense creative. Going further (in an attempt to refute Tolstoy's charge that Shakespeare's plays have no religious content) he spoke of 'the purgatorial vision of *King Lear*' and even saw Lear as analogous to the crucified Christ (Knight, 1930, 1934).

Both these parallels have been pursued by others with varying degrees of confidence. John Holloway (1961; excerpted in Kermode, 1969) pointed out that the Job parallel is sustained by Lear's own many references to the need for patience, from the opening scenes ('You heavens, give me that patience, patience I need' [II.iv.266], through the storm ('I will be the pattern of all patience' [III.ii.37], to the point where he preaches to Gloucester, 'Thou must be patient' [VI.vi.179] – unnecessarily, since Gloucester has already decided 'Henceforth I'll bear/Affliction till it do cry out itself/"Enough, enough", and die' [IV.vi.75–6]. Yet for Holloway, as for Ruth Nevo (1972), this does not lead to a facile optimistic view of the benefits of suffering: the protracted and undeserved nature of Job's sufferings constitutes a challenge to divine order and justice rather than a straightforward affirmation of it. At the extreme of scepticism, Jan Kott (1965; excerpted in Kermode, 1969) sees *King Lear* as a parody of the Job story: the book of Job performed by clowns who do not even know that they are clowns.

Other critics have been able to read the parallels more positively. Oscar James Campbell (1948), John F. Danby (1952) and James P. Driscoll (1977) all claim that Lear's journey through suffering is a salvation narrative and that patience is a redeeming factor. All three idealise Cordelia in the opening scene as a Christ-like sacrificial figure whose suffering precedes and is a pattern for Lear's.

Apart from allowing Lear and Gloucester to exhibit the virtue of patience (which, it must surely be admitted, they do only sporadically and when they have little option), it is frequently claimed that their suffering constitutes an educational experience, bringing them greater knowledge and insight than they had before. It is difficult to know what kind of knowledge is intended: certainly they learn enough to reverse their initial judgements about the merits of their children, and they learn that the distribution of wealth is difficult and unfair, but these revelations are not exactly shattering and it is very hard to believe so much suffering was necessary to achieve them.

Paul A. Jorgensen (1967) usefully provides a context of other Renaissance discussions of the theme of *self*-knowledge, demonstrating its importance both in moral treatises and in other works of fiction. He does conclude that Lear is engaged in a process of discovering his own identity, aided by the Fool, and that the various other characters act as foils to him, but he also acknowledges that 'this is a play in which the questions are greater than the answers' (p. 115) and that the extent of Lear's success is questionable. Others have disputed even this degree of optimism: Barbara Everett (1960; reprinted in Kermode, 1969) thinks Lear learns little that is novel or important, and A. L. French (1972) uses iv.vi to demonstrate that Lear is still blaming other people for his problems, still yearning for power, still totally self-centred when he isn't merely nihilistic: his 'insight' is partial and fitful at best.

In an interesting study of the whole concept of 'tragic knowledge' as some kind of compensation for suffering, Thomas P. Roche, Jr. (1981), is properly sceptical about the motives behind it, pointing out that 'It is an attractive theory because it allows each viewer or hearer to let the hero off on whatever grounds he chooses, granting to the hero whatever knowledge the critic brings to the play' (pp. 140–1). He is dubious whether the concept is relevant to any of Shakespeare's tragedies, least of all *King Lear*, finding Lear's condition at the end 'a more battered version of the ignorance he displayed at the beginning' (p.157).

Finally, it seems worth noting that nobody in the play apart from Edgar comments on either the redemptive or the educational value of suffering. Good characters such as Albany and Cordelia are utterly shocked when they hear of what is happening to Lear and Gloucester. Albany is moved to anger and contempt for the perpetrators (though both his longer speeches on this theme in iv.ii are cut in the Folio), while Cordelia is moved to sorrow [iv.iii and iv.iv]. Both are in total sympathy with the sufferers, and we should no doubt find it both inept and offensive if they qualified that sympathy with some version of Regan's comment, 'to wilful men/The injuries that they themselves procure/Must be their schoolmasters' [ii.iv.297–9]. At the end we must agree with Kent that the most important thing about the suffering is that it should stop: deterring Edgar from his presumably futile attempt to revive Lear, he says, 'O, let him pass. He hates him/That would upon the rack of this tough world/Stretch him out longer' [v.iii.311–13].

The ending

Our response to the ending of the play will of course be seriously affected by whether we accept or reject Christian readings. Some critics who are anxious to stress positive qualities – the affirmation of love, the reunion of fathers and children, the salvation of Lear and Gloucester – conveniently neglect to mention the last scene at all; the ending is 'whisked away', as H. A. Mason puts it in his discussion of L. C. Knights (Mason, 1970, p. 168). But others (including Christians) have wrestled with numerous problems. Not only is there the apparently gratuitous death of Cordelia, but there is also the uncertain state of Lear's own mind at the moment of his death, and the long string of complications and reversals which are a feature of the last scene up to the enigmatic closing lines. On one side we find critics talking about a sense of renewal, transcendence and consolation (for example Knight, 1930; Danby, 1949; Muir, 1952; and Knights, 1959); on the other side critics talking about disintegration, annihilation and total negation (for example Stampfer, 1960; Brooke, 1964; and French, 1972).

Critical expectations and emphases change according to the assumptions we make about the world outside the play. Johnson objected that 'Shakespeare has suffered the virtue of Cordelia to perish in a just cause, contrary to the natural ideas of justice' (1765; excerpted in Kermode, 1969, pp. 28–9). His response is dominated, as Norman N. Holland has demonstrated (1978), by the issue of 'justice' and he deplores its absence, whereas for some of the most recent commentators it is precisely the fact that the death is unjust, arbitrary and accidental which makes it powerful. Ruth Nevo writes that 'Nothing could more intensify the obdurate fact of tragic existence than the tension between the inevitable and the merely untimely in the final outcome' (1972, p. 303), and Susan Snyder agrees that Cordelia's death is most moving, not because it is 'undeserved' but because it seems merely due to bad timing (1979, p. 157).

Lear's death is problematic in a different way. Bradley's claim that Lear dies thinking Cordelia is alive, that he has succeeded in saving her, and that consequently 'the agony in which he actually dies is one not of pain but of ecstasy' (1904; excerpted in Kermode, 1969, pp. 102–3), has been much disputed (see summaries of the arguments in Walton, 1960; and Peat, 1980). It is certainly quite extraordinary that Shakespeare does not make it clear beyond critical dispute whether Lear is supposed to see signs of life or signs of death on Cordelia's lips as he dies crying, 'Look there! Look there!' [v.iii.309]. It is equally extraordinary that, unlike Shakespeare's other tragic heroes, he has no final moment of self-consciousness, he makes no attempt to sum up his experiences or to direct the responses of the bystanders. He dies rather, as Maynard Mack puts it, with '[his] whole consciousness launched towards another' (1965; excerpted in Muir, 1984, p. 223): he is utterly preoccupied with Cordelia and does not seem even to acknowledge that he himself is dying. In real life, many people die without knowing they are dying, but in dramatic tragedy it is extremely unusual for the hero to pass in this way.

The bystanders, perhaps significantly, react in different ways. Albany makes the conventional gesture (already begun at l. 294 but interrupted(!) by the death of Lear) of trying to dispose the future, suggesting a triumvirate rule or perhaps even another division of the kingdom between himself, Kent and Edgar, but Kent declines, indicating that he will follow his master, and Edgar speaks the final difficult lines:

The weight of this sad time we must obey;
Speak what we feel, not what we ought to say.
The oldest hath borne most; we that are young
Shall never see so much nor live so long.

[v.iii.321–4]

This is, to say the least, puzzling. What does it mean to 'obey the weight of the time'? What is it that Edgar 'ought to say' in contrast to what he feels? How can he *know* that he will not 'see so much nor live so long' as Lear? Editors and critics have struggled with these lines, finding in them a note of apology (Hunter, 1972), an element of sombre optimism (Duthie, 1960) or sheer exhaustion (Shaw, 1966). Most people seem to feel they are somehow appropriate: a more normal ending, one that included, for example, the usual indication that the characters will now repair to some other location, would undermine the effect.

Perhaps predictably, several critics have responded to one or more of the difficulties outlined above by stressing the ambiguous or mixed nature of the ending. John D. Rosenberg (1966) tried to arbitrate between the 'redemptivist' position and the 'nihilist' position, advocating one which was capable of holding both elements in tension. Similarly for S. L. Goldberg (1974), Michael Long (1976) and Derek Peat (1980), the key to the ending is in oscillation, uncertainty, and the interdependence of contraries. It is true that Lear oscillates between hope and despair in his final speech and that, in a different way, Gloucester's heart ''Twixt two extremes of passion, joy and grief,/Burst smilingly' [v.iii.196–7], so it can be claimed that the apparently contradictory views of the critics merely echo the oscillations of the play itself and that the ending contains both renewal and disintegration, both redemption and absurdity. S. L. Bethell (1944) and Peter Davison (1982) have illustrated through their insistence on 'multiconscious apprehension' that such contradictory views can be held simultaneously by the audience.

The problems can also be seen in generic or structural terms. The play's similarities to comedy or romance, discussed above, provide a constant but ultimately false hope that yet another reversal can take place, that there really is a chance that Cordelia might be saved (see McNeir, 1969; Reibetanz, 1977). At the same time the complexity of the double plot structure can appear to be a cause of the problems: Bradley found the ending lacking in dramatic clearness partly because of the sheer number of loose ends that need to be tied up, and H. A. Mason agreed, calling the last act 'a fine cathedral surrounded by slums' (1970, p. 219), but Emrys Jones has argued that it is entirely appropriate that the last scene should be structured by the irruption of chance and should have a tendency to get lost in the clogging detail which is characteristic of the whole play (1971, p. 192).

The ending is indeed formally eccentric in a number of ways. Susan Snyder points out that, although Lear does not acknowledge his own death, there is a sense in which the death of Cordelia allows him 'to do the impossible, to experience his own death' (1984, p. 459), while Carol Marks (1968) notes that the final summing up or eulogy, which normally comes after the major characters have died, is anticipated in, or replaced by Lear's 'Upon such sacrifices, my Cordelia,/The gods themselves throw incense' [v.iii.20–1]. Stephen Booth, in a full and very subtle discussion of the whole problem (1983), sees *King Lear* as a play which deliberately refuses ordinary forms of closure: it 'ends but does not stop' (p. 11). This is a matter not just for the characters but also for the audience, who must likewise 'cope with the fact that the idea of the ultimate is *only* an idea' (p. 12). Booth finds the play a triumph of both endurance or duration and of indefiniteness or 'indefinition': it is particularly demanding because the anticipated conclusion is delayed and ultimately withheld.

Approaches to staging and performance

There is a curiously persistent tradition, despite much argument and many productions to the contrary, that *King Lear* is not an effective play in the theatre. Charles Lamb famously wrote that 'Lear is essentially impossible to be represented on a stage. . . . To see Lear acted, to see an old man tottering about the stage with a walking-stick, turned out of doors by his daughters in a rainy night, has nothing in it but what is painful and disgusting' (1812; excerpted in Kermode, 1969, pp. 44–5). A century later A. C. Bradley seemed to agree when he wrote of *King Lear* as 'Shakespeare's greatest achievement . . . but *not* his best play' (1904; excerpted in Kermode, 1969, p. 83), and more recently still Margaret Webster, writing as an experienced actress and director, described it as 'the least actable' of the major tragedies (1957, p. 214).

None of these critics is hostile to the play; rather it is because their estimation of it as a text is so high that they feel no theatrical representation can be adequate. Lamb insisted that 'The greatness of Lear is not in corporal dimension, but in intellectual. . . . On the stage we see nothing but corporal infirmities and weakness.' Bradley found *Lear* 'too huge for the stage', and Webster said that the actors and the audience are 'strained beyond the limits of the theatre medium'. *King Lear* should, it is assumed, be a sublime experience, but in reality it is more likely to be tedious or even ridiculous.

Stage history

Does the actual stage history of the play support these views? Shakespeare was undoubtedly a practical man of the theatre, actor as well as writer and shareholder, whose expertise we might be prepared to respect, as Harley Granville-Barker, another man of the theatre, argues in his defence of the play against Bradley and others (1946; excerpted in Muir, 1984). Unfortunately, we have no evidence that *King Lear* was particularly successful in Shakespeare's own time. Records of performances are sparse, though this is not unusual and need not carry much weight. Other indications are, if anything, negative: some of the Folio cuts (for example, Lear's 'trial' of his daughters in III.vi) *may* have been made because the audience laughed inappropriately, and *The Shakespeare Allusion Book* lists very few references to *Lear* in the works of other writers – even *Pericles* and *The Merry Wives of Windsor*, let alone the other tragedies, were mentioned more often (see Hunter, New Penguin Shakespeare edn., 1972, p. 46).

Notoriously, Shakespeare's text was not performed at all for a century and a half after 1681, when Tate's adaptation held the stage. While retaining some long passages of Shakespeare's dialogue, Tate added a love affair between Cordelia and Edgar (who saves her from being abducted and raped by Edmund), omitted the Fool, and, as I have said above, provided a happy ending in which Lear and Gloucester both survive, Lear is restored to the throne but retires (with Kent) to a life of meditation, leaving Cordelia and Edgar to a harmonious rule. This would have been the version seen by Lamb, though he and William Hazlitt put pressure on Edmund Kean to restore the tragic ending, which he did in 1823. The Fool did not return to the stage until Macready's production of 1838, when the part was played by a woman. Even in the mid nineteenth century, in Charles Kean's 1858 production as well as in Macready's, major passages such as the blinding of Gloucester and his attempted suicide were omitted.

Practical problems have always beset the staging of *King Lear*. Shakespeare's bare stage was pre-eminently flexible but, as the theatre became more concerned with naturalistic illusion, the settings and special effects became more and more elaborate. In the nineteenth century, the fashion was for settings which were authentically primitive but at the same time romantic and spectacular. Vast naturalistic castles and monolith-strewn heaths were constructed as archaeological realism vied with scenic splendour. The storm scenes seemed equally problematic with or without machinery: either the actors' voices were drowned out by the noise or they seemed to be railing against a purely imaginary tempest. One reason for the omission of Gloucester's suicide attempt (it became customary for Lear to enter early and interrupt this episode) was presumably that the scene itself challenges the conventions of the naturalistic theatre by having Edgar describe so graphically a cliff which is not in fact present.

Of course the archaic settings also served to highlight the play's inconsistencies and anachronisms. What are dukes and earls, a Machiavellian villain (Edmund), a Bedlam beggar and a Renaissance court fool (when he was allowed to appear) doing at Stonehenge or in an ornate Anglo-Saxon palace? Why do they keep talking about tailors and taverns, and how does such a primitive society manage to have such an extraordinarily swift and efficient system for the delivery of messages and letters? The more 'authentic' the play appeared to be in a historical sense, the more problematic it became.

The twentieth century

Twentieth-century critics have been as dismissive of nineteenth-century productions as of the 'Tatefied' *Lear* which preceded them, condemning with Maynard Mack the 'archaeological impulse of the nineteenth-century stage to convert poetry and myth into history' (1965; excerpted in Kermode, 1969, p. 65). As he says, the result was to mask the play's archetypal character and to allow the audience a comfortable sense of distance and superiority. The modern stage is no longer subject to the tyranny of naturalism, perhaps because our requirements in this area are satisifed much more fully by cinema and television. Any attempt the theatre can make to evoke a real storm today is going to look inadequate beside what the camera can do, and so the theatre is, perhaps mercifully, freed from the obligation to make the attempt in the first place. Conversely, it is in the cinema that the struggle to produce convincingly primitive-looking *King Lears* still goes on: in recent years Peter Brook, Grigori Kozintsev and Akira Kurosawa have all felt obliged to give the play a consistently archaic setting, and Kozintsev omitted Gloucester's suicide attempt, presumably agreeing with Jan Kott (1965; excerpted in Kermode, 1969) as well as with nineteenth-century producers that it is an essentially theatrical event, not possible in a naturalistic context. (I shall have more to say about these film versions below.)

Modern critics have made a self-conscious attempt to reclaim *King Lear* for the theatre. Following Granville-Barker, many critics have argued against Bradley while others have simply taken it for granted that there is no longer any need to do so. All recent editors assume that the text, although very demanding, can be acted. Indeed it has become orthodoxy to insist that the play can *only* be fully realised on the stage. The most ambitious and detailed statement of this position is in Marvin Rosenberg's *The Masks of King Lear* (1972): his method is to juxtapose critical interpretation against theatrical interpretation in a scene-by-scene analysis of the play. The method is laborious and exhaustive (the analysis of the first scene takes seventy pages), but the reader can hardly help being impressed with the almost endless range of possibilities offered and the evidence of so many enthusiastic interpreters.

In a more piecemeal way, other critics have examined the ways in which Shakespeare offers both help and rewards for actors who undertake this play. Michael Goldman has an interesting essay (1981) on what he calls 'histrionic imagery' in *King Lear*. By this he means 'motifs of enactment: mental, physical and emotional movements the actor is called upon to make that are particularly related to his basic work of sustaining the part in performance' (p. 25). In detail, he argues that the performer of the role of Lear is assisted in his task of sustaining vivid and exact emotions by the way in which Shakespeare repeatedly encourages him to focus on a specific sensation (the prick of a pin, the pressure of a button, the wetness of tears) or a specific object (Gloucester's eyes, Cordelia's mouth). In a somewhat similar vein, P. W. Thomson writes enthusiastically about the sheer pleasure an actor can get from playing such a role as Lear (or for that matter Edmund or Edgar), partly because of the further levels of role play demanded (1983), and Pierre Sahel enumerates the many play metaphors, images of the theatre, and play-within-the play devices which help to make *King Lear* supremely 'theatrical' (1983).

But above all there has been in recent years a widespread sense that *King Lear* might almost have been written for the twentieth-century stage. This is because of recent events both inside and outside the theatre. Writing about his production of the play with the San Francisco Actors' Workshop in 1961, Herbert Blau remarked, 'The setting cuts back behind history, but it also extends to the twentieth century with its saturation bombings, human lampshades, incinerators and hydrogen bombs' (1963). A year later, in England, Peter Brook's production was seen as an existential interpretation for a post-nuclear age. Both these productions were discussed by Maynard Mack in his extremely influential *'King Lear' in Our Time* (1965; excerpted in Kermode, 1969, and in Muir, 1984), in which he considered those aspects of the play which 'give it particular immediacy and impact for twentieth-century sensibilities'. He claimed that the 'tragic heroic' content of *King Lear*, 'like that of most contemporary plays, is ambiguous and impure'. Death is not noble but 'miscellaneous and casual', a mere release from suffering, something to which 'the generations that have known Hiroshima are attuned' (p. 223 in Muir). Those generations are also, of course, well able to respond, though in a different way from the Jacobean audience, to the idea of the literal end of the world.

At much the same time, in Poland, Jan Kott published *Shakespeare Our Contemporary* (1965) with the chapter I have already referred to called '*King Lear*, or Endgame'. This essay, which had previously been published in Polish and in French, had already influenced Peter Brook's production (see Marowitz, 1963; Styan, 1977; and Salgado, 1984). Confirming the immediate appeal for modern audiences, Kott, as I have said, emphasised the grotesque or absurd elements in the play and, like Mack, associated them with the contemporary drama of Brecht, Dürrenmatt and Beckett. Writing of the enormous influence that Shakespeare has had on European drama he remarks that '[the] theatres in which Shakespeare's plays have been produced, were in turn influenced by contemporary plays. Shakespeare has been a living influence in so far as contemporary plays, through which his dramas were interpreted, were a living force themselves' (Kott, 1965, p. 103). Thus the influence is in effect mutual. Not only is the world of the play, in which 'fate, gods and nature have been replaced by history' recognisable today, but its mode of presentation can now be seen as anti-naturalist in a modernist way: 'The exposition of *King Lear* seems preposterous if one is to look in it for psychological verisimilitude. . . . It is absurd' (pp. 102–3).

Thus both the political events of the twentieth century, especially the Second World War and the invention of the atom bomb, and the development of a particular kind of theatre can be seen as having produced audiences receptive to those aspects of *King Lear* which had seemed to previous generations too extreme, too cruel, too improbable or too ludicrous.

Peter Brook's production was, to say the least, controversial. It was enormously successful with the theatre-going public (when it transferred from Stratford to London every seat for the entire run was sold before it opened), but academic reviewers in particular complained about the coldness and drabness of the production and the apparent attempt to expunge any heroism or even dignity from the text. Going to the opposite extreme from Tate's imposition of a happy ending, Brook had made the play as bleak as possible. Most famously, he omitted the two servants at the end of III.vii who, after the blinding of Gloucester, do their best to help him, and deliver some moral judgements on Regan and Cornwall. Brook's Gloucester was simply pushed aside and left to grope about the stage on his own for some moments after the full house lights had come up for the interval. This cut could have been justified on textual grounds (the lines are omitted from the Folio), but, as Charles Marowitz, the assistant director, explained in 'Lear Log' (1963), his detailed record of the production, it was done on this occasion 'to remove the tint of sympathy usually found at the end of the blinding scene' (pp. 28–9).

Maynard Mack, who quotes this argument in *'King Lear' in Our Time*, objects vigorously to what he sees as the diminution or reduction of the text by the determination to emphasise one aspect of it at the expense of the whole, and Robert Speaight, reviewing the production for *Shakespeare Quarterly* in 1963, criticises the Stratford directors for 'asking the question "What can Shakespeare mean to us?" before asking the more important question, "What did Shakespeare himself intend?"' (reprinted in Muir, 1984, p. 279).

How far should directors of Shakespeare go in pursuit of 'relevance'? Alan Sinfield raises this question again in relation to the 1982 Royal Shakespeare Company season at Stratford, when Adrian Noble's production of *King Lear* was playing in the main theatre alongside Barry Kyle's production of Edward Bond's *Lear* at the Other Place, the studio theatre (Sinfield, 1982). While expressing considerable enthusiasm for Bond's *Lear* (which had first been performed in 1971) as an explicit and independent critique of Shakespeare's play, Sinfield has problems with Adrian Noble's obvious intentions to bring out a contemporary political dimension in *King Lear* itself. He finds the result politically confused and traces this confusion to the double influences of Brecht and Beckett which still prevail in British theatre. As he points out, these influences are in some ways incompatible: Brecht was explicitly political and materialist, essentially optimistic in locating evil in potentially changeable social structures, whereas Beckett is apolitical, absurdist, even nihilist. This combination of influences worked somehow in the hands of Peter Brook in 1962, but, Sinfield argues, will no longer work today.

Moreover, Sinfield questions both the motivation and the likely success of attempts to 'ventriloquise a modern political stance through the play' (p. 14). He assumes that we want to do this because our conception of the greatness of *King Lear* depends upon its ability to speak to all conditions (an assumption I shall take up again in Part Two), so the play would lose its authority if we were to admit that it is a basically conservative text which has very little of relevance to say to left-wing intellectuals at the time of the Falklands war. If we force it to become relevant through indiscriminate cutting and stage business, the resulting production will inevitably be confused by countervailing implications still left in the text. This essay is written from a very different position from that adopted in the 1960s by Mack and Speaight, but the plea for a greater degree of honesty in facing the text for what it is seems comparable.

Film and television

The majority of people today are more likely to see *King Lear* in the cinema or on television rather than in the theatre, and British audiences have had the opportunity to see three film versions and three television versions made since 1970, attesting to the continuing prestige and popularity of the play as well as to a fair degree of confidence in its stageability, or rather screenability.

Two of the film versions were made at the same time: Peter Brook and Grigori Kozintsev, the Soviet director who had already made a celebrated film of *Hamlet* (1964), met in Paris in 1967 and discussed their plans for filming *King Lear*. Kozintsev had seen Brook's stage version when it toured the Soviet Union, and the two men were enthusiastic about each other's work. They began shooting at the same time, Brook in northern Jutland, Kozintsev in the Crimea, and exchanged a number of letters about their problems, theories and

experiences, some of which Kozintsev subsequently published
in his book *'King Lear': The Space of Tragedy* (1973, English tr.
1977). Both films were released in 1970, though Kozintsev's
was not seen in the West until it was premièred at the World
Shakespeare Congress in Vancouver in August 1971.

Brook and Kozintsev agreed in choosing a primitive 'look'
and in making their films in wild but non-specific locations.
They both chose to use black and white rather than colour,
and they made extensive use of close-ups. They tried to find
visual equivalents for the metaphorical language of the play
while on the whole avoiding 'Hollywood' style spectacle. Of
course there were differences in their interpretations: Brook
was still working under the influences of Kott and Beckett
(though these were less marked than in his 1962 stage
version), while Kozintsev saw the play as a sort of Christian–
Marxist parable about irresponsible rulers and the unfair
distribution of wealth. He was also influenced by the epic
style in Russian film-making; the large numbers of beggars
who fill the screen in his *Lear* are reminiscent of similar
crowds in such films as Eisenstein's *Ivan the Terrible*.

Both Brook and Kozintsev were highly impressed with the
film version of *Macbeth*, known in England as *The Throne of
Blood* (or *Cobweb Castle*), made by the Japanese director Akira
Kurosawa in 1957. Recently, in 1985, Kurosawa's version of
King Lear, called *Ran* (meaning 'chaos') was released to
considerable acclaim, especially in the West. It is a complete
contrast, both to his own *Macbeth* film and to the other two
Lear films, revelling in colour and spectacle with a cast of
thousands, elaborate costumes, huge battle scenes and an
equally huge budget. It is also very different from the films
by Brook and Kozintsev in its very free adaptation of the text;
indeed Kurosawa has regularly claimed that *Lear* was only a
secondary source of *Ran*, which is primarily based on a
sixteenth-century Japanese story (see Raison and Toubiana,
1985). For many viewers, it confirmed an assumption that
film versions are more likely to be successful in their own
terms the bolder they are about leaving the text behind and
offering themselves as adaptations rather than faithful
interpretations. In this respect *Ran* makes an interesting
comparison with Edward Bond's *Lear*.

Television versions made in Britain have not exploited this

sort of freedom. Moreover the medium itself, with its small screen and its preference for 'talking heads' seems inappropriate for any Renaissance play, let alone one on the scale of *King Lear*. Nevertheless the play was of course included in the recent complete BBC Shakespeare series, in a version directed by Jonathan Miller in 1982, and it was also directed for Granada television by Michael Elliott in 1984. (Miller had previously directed the play with the same principal actors for BBC television in 1975.) The two versions are very different: Elliott set his star, the elderly and frail Laurence Olivier, in a quasi-naturalistic landscape, beginning at Stonehenge and moving to real woodland in which, at his first appearance in iv.vi, Olivier caught, skinned and apparently ate a real rabbit. Miller's production took place on a virtually bare set, though the costumes were decidedly Jacobean. His Lear, Michael Hordern, was boisterous and violent, contrasting strongly with the sweetness and gentleness of Olivier's performance. Clearly the debate over *how* to stage or film *King Lear* continues, while the debate over whether it *can* be staged has become more muted.

Specialised approaches, key words, scenes and metaphors

Introducing a collection of critical essays on *King Lear* in 1984, Kenneth Muir remarks that during the twentieth century criticism has become more specialised: 'Although there have been notable attempts to provide an overall view of the play, most books and articles are devoted to more limited topics' (1984, p. xii). This is hardly surprising, given the difficulty, in criticism as in performance, of doing justice to every single aspect of the play, however desirable that might be in theory. In practice every work of criticism, like every performance, is bound to be selective and partial, highlighting some elements of the play at the expense of others.

Many of the works I have already discussed could be described as specialist in this sense, since they concentrate on the text, the religious background or whatever. As it happens they fitted in more conveniently elsewhere in my organisational scheme, though they could have been discussed here. What I shall do in this section is consider some specialised approaches which did not fit in elsewhere, and, more importantly perhaps, consider what might be termed 'microlevel' approaches – ones which concentrate on a small area, perhaps a single character, theme, scene, speech, metaphor, or even a single word. These approaches seem to be particularly valuable for two reasons. First, it can be very liberating to avoid or at least postpone the rather awesome obligation to provide 'an overall view of the play'; and, secondly, such approaches are more within the range of what most of us, as students or teachers of *King Lear*, can actually undertake for ourselves. Of course, as with the other sections, I can only cover a small, but I hope not unrepresentative, range of the possible approaches.

Language

A popular and important specialised approach is the one through 'imagery'. Since the pioneering work of Caroline F. E. Spurgeon (1935) and Wolfgang Clemen (1951), many studies have been published. Spurgeon found *King Lear* to be dominated by two particular groups of images: ones drawn from the human body and its movements (often painful or violent) and ones drawn from the animal world. Clemen explored the ways in which these images (especially the animal ones) are integrated into the structure of the play and the interrelationships amongst the characters. The most ambitious study in this tradition is, however, Robert B. Heilman's *This Great Stage: Image and Structure in 'King Lear'* (1948), which, as the title implies, examines the structure of the play through its images, discussing the patterns of references to sight, smell, clothes, sex, animals and justice. Like Clemen, Heilman goes beyond identifying images to argue for their contribution to the organic unity of the play. Some hostile critics, for example W. R. Keast (1949) and Paul J. Alpers (1962), attack Heilman not so much on the existence or importance of the images he discusses as on the question of how precisely to interpret them. Keast rejects the way in which Heilman makes the imagery patterns serve an essentially Christian, even optimistic, reading of the play, while Alpers rejects the traditional interpretation of the 'sight' pattern, arguing that it has more to do with human feeling and recognition than with moral insight. Heilman's book has nevertheless been accepted as a standard work and has been followed by a vast number of essays on particular aspects of the play's 'imagery': the Garland Bibliography (Champion, 1980) lists around 100 items published between 1940 and 1978.

The approach through 'imagery' has, however, frequently been challenged by those who feel it lacks an adequate methodology or that it is inappropriate to dramatic texts: see Foakes (1952), Muir (1965), and Weimann (1974). I myself have recently written a book with John O. Thompson (1987) in which we argue that some approaches to metaphor developed recently outside literary studies, mainly in linguistics and philosophy, might be more productive; we have one chapter in which we apply one of these approaches to animal metaphors in *King Lear*.

There have been other ways of talking about the language of *King Lear*. At the opposite extreme from the imagery critics, who are usually most interested in the richest and most complex moments in the text, some people have examined its more mundane aspects. Winifred Nowottny (1960) finds the language of *King Lear* 'flat and grey' compared with that of the other tragedies, deliberately lacking in 'poetic' effects. It is powerful not because it deviates from everyday language but because it exploits it. The virtues of blunt, plain speech are thematised in the play (for example, in Kent's persona as Caius and, of course, in Cordelia's refusal to use the ornate language of flattery), and some of its most important moments are couched in natural, prosaic language, even to the ending where Lear laments the death of Cordelia in 'the terms of common grief' (p. 56). A similar emphasis on the ordinary, everyday basis of the play's language is found in Rosalie L. Colie's discussion of a series of commonplace paradoxes in it (1966).

Syntax can also be significant. Nowottny, again, claims, in an essay called 'Lear's Questions' (1957), that the mood of the play is essentially interrogative: Lear in particular is always asking questions, and the basic one, 'What is Man?'

underlies the whole play. This, she says, puts the emphasis on revelation through suffering rather than redemption through suffering. Madeleine Doran has also written on the prevalence of commands, questions and assertions in *King Lear* (1976), and Alessandro Serpieri (1979) has analysed the use of comparative terms in the opening scene, claiming that this grammatical feature points to much larger issues: the systematically hierarchical society of the play depends for its very existence on the assumption that patterns of more and less, better and worse, are not only proper but divinely sanctioned. Cordelia's refusal to ask for more than her sisters by comparing her love favourably with theirs constitutes a threat to this system and leaves her, Lear, Edgar and Kent in danger of becoming 'nothing'.

Narrowing the focus to individual words, in *The Structure of Complex Words* (1951) William Empson has a fascinating chapter, 'Fool in *Lear*', in which he explores the whole issue of foolishness, folly and related concepts in this play, which he calls 'the supreme exercise-ground of the word *fool*' (p. 125). Terence Hawkes (1959; reprinted in Kermode, 1969) has written on Shakespeare's use of different senses of the word 'love'.

Scenes

Serpieri is not alone in focusing his discussion on a single significant scene. Other critics have employed this approach either within a longer analysis of the play or as the basis of an independent study. Of those already mentioned in previous sections, critics who are particularly notable for their attention to each scene of the play as a separate unit are Emrys Jones (1971) and Marvin Rosenberg (1972). As is indicated by his title, *Scenic Form in Shakespeare*, Jones is concerned with structural analysis, both of individual scenes and of groups of scenes. He finds models for many of the scenic patterns in *King Lear* in Shakespeare's own earlier work, especially the *Henry VI* plays, *King John* and *As You Like It*. Rosenberg, on the other hand, employs the scene-by-scene method mainly for convenience in his extensive juxtaposition of critical and theatrical interpretations. As I have said, he spends a long time on the opening scene, which has also been widely discussed by a number of critics with varying special interests: the sources, the setting, the themes, the question of improbability, the topical and political implications, the characters of Lear and Cordelia, and so on. There are in fact few discussions of *King Lear* of any length which do *not* have something to say about the opening scene.

Less attention has been paid to some of the climatic moments later in the play. Gary Taylor has recently, however, devoted some seventy pages to an analysis of Lear's traumatic confrontation with Goneril in i.iv (1985). He is particularly concerned to assess the theatrical impact of this scene, which moves from Lear's impression of 'a most faint neglect' in the attitudes of Goneril and her servants to his violent repudiation of Goneril herself and his impetuous departure from her house. This scene is more obviously central to the dramatic narrative than iv.vi, which is analysed by Harry Levin (1959; reprinted in Muir, 1984). While it begins with an important event (or rather non-event) in the form of Gloucester's attempted suicide, and ends with a little flurry of plot in the delivery of news of the impending battle and Edgar's killing of Oswald, which leads to the discovery of the incriminating letter from Goneril to Edmund, the bulk of this long scene does not particularly forward the narrative at all, consisting as it does of the strange, painful meeting of the mad Lear and the blind Gloucester. Levin argues that it is nevertheless the culmination of the pattern of references in the play to sight, insight and recognition.

Themes

Thematic approaches have been much more common than scenic ones, and again many of the works discussed in previous sections employ a thematic approach. Here I should like to mention just a couple of the play's themes which have perhaps not had as much attention as they deserve.

I have been surprised to find that relatively little has been said directly about Lear's madness. An essay by Kenneth Muir (1960) usefully compares Shakespeare's treatment of madness in the play with the ways in which other dramatists of the time depicted mad people (usually, as it happens, with considerable sympathy and seriousness). He relates it to contemporary medical theory and traces its development in the play. Josephine Waters Bennett (1962) sees Lear's madness as an important means of intensifying and clarifying the play's meaning, at the same time taking a strong moral line as she sees it as an index of the extent of Lear's guilt for the state of his society and chides Bradley for his over-sympathetic attitude. Most recently, E. A. J. Honigmann's essay 'Lear's Mind' (1976) considers more generally the importance to the play of Lear's peculiar and shifting mental perspectives and of the audience's need to adjust to the vagaries of his condition.

While the theme of justice has been discussed more than once (see, for example, Sisson, 1962; excerpted in Kermode, 1969), the opposite concept of anarchy, upside-downness or topsy-turvydom has been highlighted in two recent articles by James Black (1980) and Theodore Weiss (1981). Black approaches this through Shakespeare's overturning of received dramatic conventions and techniques, while Weiss sees the play as 'a mélange . . . a hurly-burly . . . a veritable refuse heap' (1981, p. 64) which thereby has a particular appeal for modern readers and audiences who are used to the miscellaneous and frenetic quality of contemporary urban life.

Characters

Character-based approaches have of course been even more popular than thematic ones. Since many discussions of the play can in some ways be seen as character studies of Lear himself, I shall limit myself here to those which approach the play through the role of a minor character. Although the character-based approach has been dismissed by recent critics as outdated and naïve, it has nevertheless received a new injection of energy from the revolution in attitudes towards the text discussed in the opening pages of this survey. Obviously enough, if it is assumed that Shakespeare deliberately revised the play, then it can be argued that he deliberately changed the roles of certain characters in the process. The most significant changes are in the role of Albany (see Warren, 1978; and Urkowitz, 1980), whose expressions of anger and contempt for what his wife and her associates are doing are severely curtailed in the Folio. Kent's role in the latter part of the play is also diminished, perhaps in order to bring Cordelia into greater prominence (Warren, 1983), while the Fool's role remains much the same length in both versions (the Folio cuts 22 lines from the Quarto but adds 32 new ones), but the character has changed slightly to become a 'more urbane and more oblique' jester (Kerrigan, 1983).

Albany had previously been the subject of a study by Leo Kirschbaum (1960), who, despite having written an important book on the textual situation (1945), ignored these issues and concentrated on what he saw as the character's growth in moral stature in the course of the play. This is in fact a rare example of a critical essay whose entire basis is challenged by new attitudes to the text. The Fool had also attracted earlier attention, most notably from Enid Welsford (1935; excerpted in Kermode, 1969, and Muir, 1984), who discussed him within her wide-ranging study of the whole tradition of the social and literary history of professional fools, and by William Empson, whose work I have mentioned earlier in this section.

But the largest number of character studies, apart from those on Lear himself, have been devoted to Cordelia. Despite her relatively few lines and her prolonged physical absence from the stage (she does not appear between i.i and iv.iv), she has been assumed to embody some of the play's most important qualities (Isenberg, 1951; Driscoll, 1977). On the other hand she has been seen as proud or priggish in the opening scene and it has been claimed that her progress from this reprehensible attitude to one of love and generosity parallels her father's development (Greenfield, 1977). Furthermore, psychoanalytical critics have been dubious about the closeness of her relationship with her father to the point of suspecting incestuous desires (Dundes, 1980; and Melchiori, 1960). Sigmund Freud himself wrote briefly on *King Lear* (1913; excerpted in Muir, 1984), associating it with other stories in which the youngest of three sisters is chosen, and arguing that at a subconscious level what is really being chosen is death. This identification of Cordelia with death has not been widely accepted, but Frank Kermode remarks, 'I cannot imagine that any good critic would be so doctrinaire as to decline all assent to Freud's beautiful reading, and I would trust none who thought it exclusively right' (1971, p. 177).

For the most part critics (not all of them men with daughters) have idealised Cordelia's apparently single-minded devotion to her father after her return from France, frequently asserting that the reunion between Lear and Cordelia in iv.vii is the most moving scene in the entire canon. But Stanley Cavell seems to have been the first person to point out that Lear's desire to be alone with his daughter, expressed so touchingly in his 'Come, let's away to prison' speech [v.iii.8–19], represents 'not the correction but the repetition of his strategy in the first scene' (1969, p. 296). Once again, Lear is simply appropriating Cordelia without thinking that she might have different and independent desires. He ignores the existence of her husband now just as he had ignored the possibility that she might love anyone other than himself in i.i.

This objection to the sentimental interpretation of Cordelia's role at the end of the play has been revived by some later critics writing from a feminist standpoint (Erickson, 1985; McLuskie, 1985), though another feminist (Novy, 1984) would prefer to put the emphasis on forgiveness and mutuality, making the point that 'there is so much sympathy with Lear at the end that it seems cold to turn from feeling with him to any further analysis of the play in terms of sex-role behaviour' (p. 162). McLuskie is equally sensitive, allowing that Lear's situation at the end is so moving that 'even the most stony-hearted feminist could not withhold her pity' (p. 102), but, as we shall see in Part Two, feminist uneasiness about the extent to which King Lear endorses patriarchal institutions is one of the few areas of doubt in the general acceptance of the play's greatness.

Part Two: Appraisal – the Greatness of *King Lear*

KING LEAR stands today in a formidable position in relation to British culture in general and to English studies in particular. Despite the doubts and the negative criticisms of earlier generations of readers, audiences and critics, it seems now to be virtually unchallenged as the greatest monument of our literature: the most admired play by the most admired writer in the English language. In this section I shall investigate this remarkable situation and consider its implications.

Why do we have such an extravagant estimate of this particular play? What are the factors which determine the literary league table and who decides on its rankings? Does anyone dissent from the consensus as to *King Lear*'s supremacy, and, if so, on what grounds? Would we expect the high reputation of the play to continue or to decline?

In order to approach, if not necessarily to answer, these questions, I shall first consider some general issues about the nature and status of 'classic' texts and the formation of literary canons. I shall then look at *King Lear* in particular and at the arguments of critics who have challenged its high estimation. This is not because I want to attack the play or to dislodge it from the pedestal on which it is currently elevated, but because those who have expressed negative views are often more explicit about what they take to be the reasons for the play's greatness than those who simply take that greatness for granted. Sometimes attacks on the play have usefully provoked explicit defences, and the fact that the ground on which these arguments are conducted shifts over time is itself significant. Finally, I shall examine some trends in very recent criticism which do not so much challenge the absolute evaluation of the play as displace the whole argument about evaluation, making it seem a less important question than it has been in the past.

The literary canon and the classic text

The words 'canon' and 'classic' both evoke notions of evaluation and hierarchy. The literary canon can be narrowly defined as that which is accepted as authentic (as for example in the context of distinguishing canonical from apocryphal works in relation to the Bible or to Shakespeare), but it is usually defined more broadly as that which is assumed to be 'good' literature, in fact the 'best' literature: that which is worth preserving and passing on from one generation to the next. The term 'classic' can sometimes be used to cover a whole canon (as when we refer to all of Greek and Latin literature as 'the classics'), or it can be a vaguely derogatory term meaning 'conventional' (as in 'That is a classic example of revenge tragedy'), but it can also be a term of high praise, applied to a work of literature which is not only in the canon but at the top of the canonical hierarchy, a 'great' work perceived as having special value for its culture.

How do canons and classics come about? There are two very different ways of approaching this question. The first, and more traditional, approach begins with the canonical or classical literary works themselves and with the assumption that they possess intrinsic qualities which make them 'good' or 'great' regardless of any external considerations. The second, more modern and more radical approach, puts less weight on the works themselves and more on the social circumstances of their production, dissemination and preservation. The underlying question here is, do we think a work such as *King Lear* is great because of some essential or absolute qualities it embodies, or do we think it is great because we have been conditioned by our society, especially by our educational institutions, into accepting this judgement? It would be surprising if the answer were not 'a bit of both' on simple empirical grounds: on the one hand, we know from our own experience that we have to be *taught* to admire classic texts such as *King Lear*, but, on the other, we are unwilling to think ourselves so lacking in independent judgement that we could be taught to like anything at all. Hence we usually prefer to see that educational process not as straight indoctrination but as a matter of being guided to a *recognition* of certain intrinsic qualities.

What arguments have been put forward by those who believe in the intrinsic or absolute merit of classic texts? The standard position is succinctly expressed by the philosopher David Hume in his 1742 essay *Of the Standard of Taste*, where he argues that there is indeed such a thing as absolute excellence in literature and that it is the *continuity* of a work's reputation which proves it. What he calls 'catholic and universal beauty', which arises from 'the relation which nature has placed between the form and the sentiment', can be deduced from 'the durable admiration which attends those works that have survived all the caprices of mode and fashion, all the mistakes of ignorance and envy' (quoted by Barbara Herrnstein Smith, 1983, p. 15). To support this, he claims that 'The same Homer who pleased at Athens two thousand years ago, is still admired at Paris and London', and he attributes any dissension to a fault in the eye of the beholder, who, if he or she does not acknowledge the superiority of the work in question, must be suffering from ignorance or envy or else is simply at the mercy of fashion.

A major problem with the assumption of intrinsic value is that it seems unduly mystifying and circular: 'universal beauty' is *proved by* 'universal acclaim' at the same time as it excites it. Some writers have however tried to be more precise about what might be meant by the 'universality' of the classic. T. S. Eliot, in what seems now a rather strange paper on the subject, *What is a Classic?*, delivered to the Virgil Society late in 1944 (Eliot, 1945), puts great stress on the notion of 'maturity': 'A classic can only occur when a civilisation is mature; when a language and literature are mature; and it must be the work of a mature mind' (p. 10). This rather static view of the circumstances under which a classic is produced might be contrasted with the more dynamic view of L. C. Knights (quoted above, p. 24) that a classic, besides being 'timeless and universal', must have 'a crucial place in its author's inner biography' and must 'mark a moment of great importance in the changing consciousness of the civilisation to which it belongs' (1959, p. 84). For Knights, who is writing with *King Lear* specifically in mind, both author and society might well be in a state of development or change, whereas for Eliot it seems that a classic can only appear when development or growth has finished.

Eliot's definition turns out in fact to eliminate Shakespeare altogether. Indeed, William Congreve's *The Way of the World* is cited as being more 'mature' than any play by Shakespeare, because it 'reflects a more mature society . . . a society more polished and less provincial' (p. 12). 'Provincial' is frequently used as a negative term by Eliot, who claims that a classic must be 'universal' in the sense of having 'an amplitude, a catholicity' in its scope. This is a major element in his definition of 'maturity', another being the matter of the author's consciousness of history – again, something Eliot finds in Virgil but not, apparently, in Shakespeare.

A different line of argument is pursued by Frank Kermode, who wrote about the subject of classic texts and their survival three times during the 1970s (1971, 1975, 1979). Both in his chapter 'Survival of the Classic' (1971) and in his book *The Classic* (1975), he puts great emphasis on universality in terms of plurality of readings: classics are those works which are especially 'patient of interpretation' (1975, p. 134); they are even 'indeterminate as to meaning, lacking any clearly delineated semantic horizon. The noise that accompanies whatever information [our] questions elicit will suggest that there is much more to be had, and that without it the information [we] have got is in some measure false' (1971, p. 176). All readings will be partial because a classic is defined by its sheer size and openness, the sense that there is 'too much of it for one person's perceptions to organize, so that the work seems, if not a chaos, at least a system of potentialities beyond one's power to actualize them' (p. 175). And these potentialities may change over time: Kermode claims that a classic such as *King Lear* is 'unaffected by time yet offering itself to be read under our particular temporal disposition' (1975, pp. 140–1).

This openness is, however, precisely what most worries those who wish to insist on the absolute and intrinsic qualities of the classic. If literary values are not constant, if many different readings can be equally 'valid', might not the result be a kind of egalitarian chaos in which *any* reading or *any* evaluation is permissible? In practice, of course, the range of interpretations and evaluations possible at any given time is subject to a number of constraints and controlled by a number of institutions.

The author himself or herself has some measure of control regarding the interpretation and evaluation of the work. He or she chooses to write a particular *kind* of work, not without some foreknowledge of who will value such a work and for what reasons. Shakespeare, for example, addressed his narrative poems, *The Rape of Lucrece* and *Venus and Adonis*, to an aristocratic patron, in the expectation of a different response from the one he would get by writing a comedy or tragedy for the public theatre. A writer today would likewise expect a book of poems to be interpreted and valued in a different way (and probably by different people) from an episode in a television soap opera. (It is worth noting in passing that financial reward may or may not coincide with critical prestige.)

Literary kinds or genres change over time and play an important role in the formation of canons. As Alastair Fowler puts it, 'Of many factors determining our literary canon, genre is surely among the most decisive. Not only are certain genres regarded *prima facie* as more canonical than others, but individual works or passages may be valued more or less highly according to their generic height' (1979, p. 100). For a long time the epic poem was regarded as the most prestigious form of literature, to be succeeded by the tragic drama. These genres are still highly respected, but they are no longer available to today's writers. Not only does the hierarchy of genres shift (but there still *is* a hierarchy, as shown in the differing status of a book of poems and a soap-opera script, 'serious' and 'pulp' fiction), but the range of genres accessible at any given time is limited.

Clearly, writers do not exist in a social vacuum. They are dependent on all sorts of institutions, such as publishing, the theatre, the film and television industries. They have to write for a paying audience or readership or obtain some kind of subsidy from private patronage, the court or the state. Many people are involved in determining, in effect, not only what is in or out of the literary canon but also by what means that canon may be read. Commissioning editors who work for publishers, directors and producers of plays and films, book-reviewers, librarians, those who award literary prizes all have their degrees of power and influence. But our educational institutions are equally important: at school and university level certain bodies of professionals (teachers, inspectors, examiners) lay down the syllabus or curriculum, determining which books, plays, poems are to be studied. Moreover, by their behaviour in the classroom and by the kinds of questions they ask in examinations, they also determine the appropriate ways in which those texts are to be read.

So how much flexibility is there in the canon? English studies has not been institutionalised as an academic discipline for very long: the study of literature used to be confined to Greek and Latin texts and it was not until the beginning of the twentieth century that 'English literature' was established as a university subject. After the best part of a century, though, we find ourselves today in the midst of a debate about the nature of the canon which has manifested itself in various forms within the last few years. In the United States in 1979 the English Institute took 'Opening Up the Canon' as the theme for its conference (see Fiedler and Baker, 1981) and in 1983 the journal *Critical Inquiry* published a special issue on 'Canons'. In Britain the Literature Teaching Politics group have investigated and challenged the literary canon as prescribed for 'O' and 'A' level examinations (see their journal *LTP* 1, 1982; and Alan Sinfield's 'Shakespeare and Education', 1985), and the topic for the 1987 annual conference of higher-education teachers of English was 'Firing the Canon'.

For the most part, the impetus behind this recent interest and activity has been a desire to enlarge the canon, to open it up to a range of works hitherto excluded, notably those written by 'minority' groups, especially women.

But has anything meanwhile been happening to the old established canon? Is it just a case of adding new works to an ever-lengthening list rather than of revaluing or even discarding old ones? It is, as Barbara Herrnstein Smith remarks in her very interesting contribution to the *Critical Inquiry* special issue on 'Canons', rather surprising that this question seems to have been neglected; indeed 'the entire problematic of value and evaluation has been evaded and explicitly exiled by the literary academy' (Smith, 1983, p. 1). While the past fifty years have seen an extraordinary proliferation of critical theories, approaches and movements (Smith lists New Criticism, structuralism, psychoanalytic criticism, reader-response criticism, reception aesthetics, speech-act theory, deconstructionism, communications theory, semiotics and hermeneutics), the emphasis has been overwhelmingly on interpretation rather than on evaluation. In so far as there is a 'crisis' in English studies today (see Widdowson, 1982), it could be seen, from a canonical viewpoint, as a kind of second-order crisis: debate centres not on what literature should be studied but primarily on what modes of interpretation are appropriate. The widespread reluctance to challenge canonical authors and preference for recycling them through the latest critical '-ism' is obvious in the proliferating series of books addressed to sixth-formers and students which explicitly claim to 'reread' all the old texts in new ways.

This essentially conservative aspect of literary and educational institutions may be surprising to some of us, and disappointing to those who would favour a more radical break with tradition. This may be partly because the debate within English studies is going on at the same time as the subject itself is under threat from external political and economic pressures: budgets are being cut, jobs are being lost, sixth-formers are being encouraged to take courses in vocational and technological subjects rather than in the arts. At such a time it is understandable that even radical critics within the system are reluctant to go too far in challenging the very basis of the subject by questioning the canon. This apparent consensus is a source of comfort to a relatively traditional critic such as Frank Kermode, who, both in 1971 and in 1979, seemed genuinely worried that the self-consciously revolutionary students of the late 1960s, as they moved into positions of power and responsibility in the 1970s, would no longer care about the survival of classic texts at all.

Meanwhile, the one area in which the traditional canon is being challenged is, again, that of sexual politics. Feminist critics are not only concerned with rediscovering and 'canonising' the works of women writers but also with reappraising the works of male writers from a feminist point of view. Women are insisting on reading *as* women rather than pretending to be men, and this is having a revisionist effect on the canon. As Lawrence Lipking puts it (again in the 'Canons' issue of *Critical Inquiry*),

> Something peculiar has been happening lately to the classics. Some of them now seem less heroic, and some of them less funny. Those 'irrelevant' scenes of cruelty to women, those obsessions with chastity and purity, those all-male debates about the nature and future of the human race, those sacrifices of feeling to duty have changed their character. Some old masters even look silly. Under the gaze of women, strong writers turn pale.   (1983, p. 79)

No one has yet been dislodged from the canon, though the position of D. H. Lawrence has been looking increasingly precarious since Kate Millett's *Sexual Politics* (1970), and such writers as Milton and Shakespeare are being treated with less reverential respect than formerly.

Thanks to feminist and other pressures it has at times become something of a struggle to preserve certain texts within the canon. On the one hand, critics find themselves apologising for certain elements within a text, such as sexual, racial or national chauvinism: they repress or rationalise such things, either minimising their significance or transferring the focus of interest to more 'neutral' or formal features of the text. On the other hand, anti-establishment critics can simply reread a text by asserting that, although it *seems* to endorse establishment ideologies, it is in fact undermining or subverting them at the same time. This approach leads most obviously to 'ironic' readings of such plays as *The Taming of the Shrew* and *Henry V*, whereby the critic argues that at some level Shakespeare did not *really* endorse male supremacy or English chauvinism, thus 'saving' an apparently recalcitrant text for the canon.

But how does all this affect *King Lear*?

Challenging the evaluation of *King Lear*

The supposition that great or classic works of art embody some kind of absolute excellence that will be immediately and universally recognised by all but barbarians is of course rendered problematic by the fact that it took a long time for *King Lear* to establish itself in the English literary canon. As I have said above in the section on 'Approaches to staging and performance', there is no evidence that it was particularly successful on stage in Shakespeare's time – indeed, Ben Jonson in the Induction to *Bartholomew Fair* in 1613 was still scolding theatre-goers who thought that Thomas Kyd's *Spanish Tragedy* and Shakespeare's *Titus Andronicus* (both plays of the late 1580s or early 1590s) were the best tragedies yet written. During the long period when Tate's adaptation held the stage it was generally agreed that his version was better, and it was not until the early nineteenth century that *King Lear* began to acquire anything like the reputation it has today.

Alfred Harbage, who traces the reception of the play from its first presentation up to 1964, attributes to the Romantic critics and poets, and to Charles Lamb in particular, the achievement of 'turning the tide' of *Lear* criticism, remarking that 'Incredible as it may seem, it is in Lamb's [1812] essay that a great work of art, already two hundred years old, receives for the first time on record unstinted and unqualified praise' (Harbage, 1966, p. 87). (And even Lamb, as we have seen, thought the play was unstageable.) Harbage argues that changing notions of tragedy – that is, changing definitions of the genre – were responsible for this, since the Restoration and the eighteenth century 'had no theory of tragedy which would shelter *King Lear* (p. 85) – a remarkable example of the triumph of institutions, both critical and generic, over individual works in the determination of the literary canon. The neoclassical taste of the period disliked the mixture of comedy and tragedy in the play and rejected the ending in which the innocent, especially Cordelia, perish along with the guilty. The Romantics however, with their commitment to intensity of feeling above all else, valued *King Lear* for the sheer power of its emotions, which they, partly because of their own religious heterodoxy, were the first to read in quasi-religious terms. Hazlitt in 1817 writes of the play in terms of faith and moral purification, and Keats in his 1818 sonnet 'On Sitting Down to Read *King Lear* Once Again' sees it as 'the fierce dispute/Betwixt damnation and impassion'd clay'. As we have already seen, the sacrificial or redemptive reading of the tragedy, most influentially stated by Bradley in 1904, continued to dominate *Lear* criticism until comparatively recent times; now, in effect, we are again seeing a rejection of 'tidy' or moralistic readings which seek in some way to explain or justify the suffering in the play, and a return to a neo-Romantic stress on the sheer intensity of the suffering, now seen from a more explicitly and grimly atheistic viewpoint.

But a few critics have challenged or resisted the comparatively recent and rapid elevation of *King Lear* to its present high position in the literary canon. Most famously, Leo Tolstoy launched a vigorous attack on Shakespeare in general and *King Lear* in particular at the beginning of this century (Tolstoy, 1903). He argues that the play is thoroughly 'unnatural' in its characterisation, motivation and sequence of events; he finds the language verbose and absurd, with the few potentially moving moments lost in a welter of pompous raving; moreover, all the characters speak the *same* language: Shakespeare lacks the ability to individuate them by their speech. Further, Tolstoy disputes Shakespeare's claim to any kind of ethical authority: he is said to have no religion, never to be in earnest, only 'playing with words'. Tolstoy goes so far as to claim that the earlier *Leir* play is more admirable (partly because it is more plausible) and that Shakespeare has perverted and destroyed its excellent qualities (as, it is claimed, he also did with the sources of *Othello* and *Hamlet*). He accounts for the continuing fame of Shakespeare as, in part, a conspiracy on the part of German critics who rejected the 'cold French drama' and had none of their own so built up Shakespeare as an alternative. That aside, the general admiration of Shakespeare must be put down to a sort of mass hypnosis or 'epidemic suggestion'; Tolstoy's list of other similar 'suggestions' includes the Crusades, the search for the Philosopher's Stone, the craze for tulip-growing in Holland, the Dreyfus case, and the theories of Charles Darwin.

Tolstoy's essay appeared as a preface (though at over 100

pages a disproportionately long one) to Ernest Crosby's *Shakespeare and the Working Classes*, which is also an attack on Shakespeare's canonical status, exposing as it does the extent to which Shakespeare usually seems to be on the side of the upper classes, despising and ridiculing the working classes, who are nevertheless, in real life, encouraged to revere him. (One might well wonder at the absence of many subsequent attacks from this position, though Elliot Krieger (1979) has been developing it in a more sophisticated form.) The 1907 reprint contains extracts from a commendatory letter by George Bernard Shaw agreeing with Tolstoy on the philosophical emptiness as well as the superficiality and snobbery of Shakespeare — a familiar line for him, though he had also written in 1901 in the Preface to his own play *Caesar and Cleopatra* that 'No man will ever write a better tragedy than *Lear*'.

If one believed in a conspiracy theory of literary canons one might say that Tolstoy's heretical opinions have been successfully suppressed by the established institutions: the essay has apparently not been reprinted since 1907 and is only available in specialist libraries. Nevertheless it has been 'refuted' a number of times, notably by G. Wilson Knight (1934) and George Orwell (1947). Frank Kermode returned to it when worrying about 'The Survival of the Classic' (1971). These defences are, as I have said, interesting because of the way they articulate the positive side of the case in a more explicit way than is otherwise found in *Lear* criticism. Wilson Knight, for example, defends the play against the charge of being implausible or unnatural by stressing its symbolic, allegorical or poetic qualities and by arguing that Tolstoy's strictures derive from the very different requirements of the naturalistic nineteenth-century novel with its desire to observe and imitate everyday life. He also claims, as I have said above, that Shakespeare's plays *are* religious, and writes of *Lear* as a 'purgatorial vision'. Orwell surmises that Tolstoy's reasons for disliking *Lear* are not the ones he states but have more to do with biographical questions: 'Is it not possible that he bore an especial enmity towards this particular play because he was aware, consciously or unconsciously, of the resemblance between Lear's story and his own?' (reprinted in Kermode, 1969, p. 155). Tolstoy writes, as he himself emphasises, as 'an old man of seventy-five', and one, moreover, who has made his own 'huge and gratuitous act of renunciation' (p. 161), having in old age renounced his estate, his title and his copyrights and made a sincere but unsuccessful attempt to escape from his privileged position and live the life of a peasant. Orwell argues that Tolstoy, like Lear, acted on mistaken motives and failed to achieve his desires.

On the other hand, Orwell is prepared to accept Tolstoy's charge that Shakespeare 'liked to stand well with the rich and powerful' and was very cautious about expressing subversive opinions. And he half agrees on the religious question – 'The morality of Shakespeare's later tragedies is not religious in the ordinary sense, and certainly is not Christian' (p. 163) – though again he relates this to Tolstoy's own much more explicit Christian commitment. But finally he argues that it is not because of the quality of his philosophy that Shakespeare has survived but because of his skill with language, a skill Tolstoy does not appreciate, partly because of not being a native speaker of English. In the end he declares, 'There is no argument by which one can defend a poem. It defends itself by surviving, or it is indefensible' (p. 167). Shakespeare is 'still there' while Tolstoy's essay 'would be forgotten altogether if Tolstoy had not also been the author of War and Peace and Anna Karenina' (p. 168).

It is in this context of the survival of classic texts that Frank Kermode discusses both Tolstoy's attack on King Lear and Orwell's defence of it (Kermode, 1971). Quoting Orwell's skeleton or sketch of the play, he points out that it is just as selective as Tolstoy's, leaving out Goneril and Regan, for example, as well as the entire sub-plot. From this, Kermode suggests, 'it seems to be true of King Lear that even after one has left a lot of it out there is plenty left to work on' (p. 169), and this leads him to his theory of the indeterminacy or openness of the classic text, mentioned above. All readings are seen as partial: 'The history of Lear criticism is a history of acceptance, avoidance, selection' (p. 172). If King Lear is to be accepted as a classic at any given time it '[has] to be made to comply with the paradigmatic requirements for a classic in that time' (p. 170). In this sense Tate's adaptation turned Shakespeare's play into an eighteenth-century classic, while modern critical readings and rereadings seek to turn it into a classic as defined by today's criteria.

Frank Kermode and Kenneth Muir both reprint Orwell's essay in their respective anthologies of *Lear* criticism, though neither reprints Tolstoy. Muir explains that there 'seemed to be no point, other than historical, in reprinting Tolstoy's strange attack on the play', and continues, in the same paragraph of his Introduction, to specify only one other 'deliberate exclusion' from his collection, namely John Middleton Murry, whose hostile chapter on *King Lear* is described as 'an aberration of an intermittently great critic, as Tolstoy's diatribe was the aberration of the greatest of novelists' (Muir, 1984, p. xvi).

Again, the particular kind of 'aberration' is of interest in this context. Murry, fully aware of the temerity of his position in attacking what is generally seen as 'the most sublime and transcendent of the tragedies' associates it with such plays as *Timon of Athens* and *Troilus and Cressida* as a diseased and obsessive work. He finds the writing itself perfunctory and weary, and explains the whole thing in biographical terms: Shakespeare was 'on the verge of madness', undergoing 'a terrible primitive revulsion against sex' (Murry, 1936, pp. 338–9). While few critics have agreed with Murry that *Lear* is 'definitely inferior to the other three "great" tragedies' (p. 337), or would go so far as to prefer, as he does, *Coriolanus*, the specific grounds for his dislike are significant, heralding as they do an increasing uneasiness, more often found in female than in male critics, with the level of linguistic violence against women found in the play, especially in Lear's extraordinarily specific and detailed cursings of his daughters and in his railing about adultery in iv.vi.

As Joyce Carol Oates argues, 'The disgust expressed in the play towards women is more strident and articulate, and far less reasonable, than the disgust expressed in *Othello* and *Hamlet* and certain of the sonnets' (1981, p. 65). Sexual loathing is not strictly justified by the plot (at least so far as Lear himself is concerned), and, while Lear exclaims against Goneril and Regan as if their behaviour towards him springs from something inherently feminine (and sexual) in their natures, they are in fact, as Oates points out, behaving more like rebellious sons in testing and rejecting their father's authority. But that is precisely where the play reveals its misogynism: Edmund's rebellion against his father, although horrific in its effects, is in a sense understandable, almost inevitable, while that of Goneril and Regan, precisely *because* they are women, is seen as deeply 'unnatural' and carries connotations of monstrosity and chaos. The play's lack of balance on sexual matters, discussed by Oates in Freudian terms (though, as she remarks, Freud's own psychology does not exactly provide a model of male–female balance), has become in recent years at least as important a criticism as its supposed lack of religion or of narrative plausibility.

Some critics have found themselves arguing for a devaluation of *King Lear*, as the result of their objections to the optimistic, Christian interpretations of the play current in the first half of this century. H. A. Mason (1970) and A. L. French (1972) stand outside this consensus, though Mason is much more explicit about the implications of his arguments for the general prestige of the play. He is mainly concerned to deny that Lear is in any way saintly or shows any signs of spiritual growth, and he further finds fault with the play structurally, accusing it of inconsistency, contrivance and loose ends. Championing Gloucester, he is highly critical of Edgar, especially in what he sees as the demeaning trick of Gloucester's attempted suicide.

French also, as I have said earlier, denies that Lear is redeemed by insight or knowledge, and questions the value of his love for Cordelia at the end, which, like Stanley Cavell (see p. 58 above) he sees as intense but by no means disinterested. In a section headed 'Some Critical Consequences' (pp. 193–205), he considers whether a denial of the redemptivist view of the play constitutes a denial of its greatness. Like Mason, he assumes that one consequence is to put greater weight on the sub-plot, which brings its own problems since he finds the sub-plot weak and awkward in some ways – indeed, he sees it as a liability rather than an asset after Act III (p. 200). Since greatness seems for French to be synonymous with unity, it might indeed be threatened by the discovery that the play is in fact uneven in its achievement, though he argues around this – 'the judgement that Shakespeare in *Lear* is sometimes at his very greatest doesn't of necessity mean that the play is all of a piece'

(p. 202) – and triumphantly ends by asserting that the play is *more* disturbing (and hence, implicitly, more acceptable as a modern tragedy) if Lear does not learn anything and is not redeemed.

French, like all the critics discussed in this section, takes it for granted that the argument about whether *King Lear* is a 'great' play, a classic, a pinnacle of the literary canon, is a crucial one, but should we necessarily accept this premise?

Displacing the value argument

The emphasis in this section will be rather different from that in the previous one, where I was discussing explicit attacks on *King Lear* by people who thought it had been overestimated by others and wished to lower its standing. Few if any contemporary critics would go so far as this, but it seems to me nevertheless that there are some underlying trends in the most recent Shakespearean criticism generally and in *Lear* studies in particular which carry important implications for the argument about value. It is not so much that contemporary critics are disputing the traditionally high evaluation of *King Lear* as that new critical procedures are displacing the whole argument about value and making it seem less central than it used to.

At all levels it seems natural to want to discuss the value of works of fiction. We ask our friends if the film or television programme they saw last night was 'any good', and we scan press reviews for value judgements to help us decide how to spend our time and money when we have the choice. But at the same time it is often the case that, once a discussion gets going, we tend to displace or postpone matters of evaluation: we *describe* the work in question as much as we judge it, and many of our comments could begin 'It was interesting because . . .' rather than 'It was good or valuable because . . .'.

Much of the professional work done by literary specialists operates in the same way. It has always been possible to investigate a text in terms of its sources, its background, its language and so on without allowing the issue of absolute value to dominate one's discussion. Sometimes this kind of work has been labelled 'scholarship' as opposed to 'criticism', which has been assumed to be more directly concerned with evaluation. But is it even the case that traditional literary criticism has really been concerned with evaluation? It is possible to argue that in Shakespeare criticism, as in literary criticism more generally, the stress has been on interpretation rather than on evaluation. There have been plenty of new readings and rereadings, but the impression is of a plurality of *approaches* rather than of a plurality of *judgements* about the merits or otherwise of individual plays.

In the mid-1960s Alfred Harbage complained about 'The Myth of Perfection' in Shakespeare studies (Harbage, 1966, pp. 23–38) whereby, compared with eighteenth- and nineteenth-century editors and adapters who were prepared to correct and revise Shakespeare when they found fault with him, twentieth-century critics prefer to 'serve the myth of perfection', not by excessive enthusiasm or rapturous superlatives, but by simple assuming that, 'because the plays are excellent, they are excellent in every way – in a word that they are *perfect*' (p. 31). As he says, it is hard to imagine modern critics 'failing to discover any excellence they hope to find', and even harder to imagine them roundly terming *Measure for Measure* a 'hateful' play, as Coleridge did (p. 32). Rather, they appoint themselves as apologists, offering ingenious explanations for anything that an 'uneducated' person might assume was incoherent, obscure, tasteless or otherwise reprehensible in the canon. The result of this is that Shakespeare criticism begins to look like an undiscriminating stream of panegyric and that students in schools and colleges are both bored and intimidated by the assumption that they are not allowed to do anything with Shakespeare except repeat received notions about why he is so wonderful.

Certainly there was an *air* of competitiveness and debate surrounding Shakespeare criticism in the mid twentieth century. Richard Levin's lively investigation of trends in the field from 1950 to 1978 has a section called 'My Theme Can Lick Your Theme' (Levin, 1979), but he claims that this argumentativeness is more apparent than real: there has in fact been a widespread tolerance on the part of critics with everything that other critics write and little real debate or disagreement on major issues. The proliferation of 'new' readings which are not really very new is ascribed by Levin to the professional pressure on academic critics to publish as much as possible and the requirement for teachers to become experts, not in knowledge but in interpretation (pp. 196–8).

So where is the underlying dissent from the myth of perfection and the cosy conspiracy of tolerance? It seems to me that there are three different areas in which the assumption of excellence in *King Lear* is implicitly being displaced: by textual critics, by feminist critics and by historical critics (both new historicists and cultural materialists). I should emphasise again that we are talking about an indirect form of dissent here: none of these groups is saying that we should drop *King Lear* from the literary canon or cease regarding it as a great or classic work, but their approaches are subtly, at times unconsciously, shifting our attitudes away from the traditional attribution of superior status.

The textual issue is, as I said at the beginning of Part One, a very basic one. It might superficially be dismissed as a merely pedantic question with no serious consequences for the critical evaluation of the play, but equally it could have some very profound effects. For one thing, it becomes much more difficult to assume that the text is perfect or excellent in every way if there is no longer any such thing as 'the text' but rather two texts with a large number of differences which can be explained in several ways. This is at least psychological shock and a circumstance which should give pause to unduly simple notions of 'greatness' as something which is intrinsic to a particular arrangement of words on a page. Which words on which page? How many words, passages, scenes need to be altered or omitted from the familiar composite text to make us feel that we are now dealing with a *different* play?

Moreover, the detailed arguments about whether the Folio is or is not Shakespeare's own revision of the Quarto have at times turned precisely on questions of artistic merit. Those arguing in favour of authorial revision have needed to claim that the Folio is *better* than the Quarto in specific ways, since Shakespeare can hardly be imagined as having deliberately made his play worse, whereas those arguing against authorial revision have claimed the opposite – namely, that some of

the changes in the Folio are so inept that they cannot
possibly have been made by Shakespeare. Thus the textual
debate drives people into making overt value judgements, at
least at the level of local passages, in place of a blanket
assumption of excellence.

Feminist doubts about *King Lear* have just come up in the
discussion of the apparently excessive nature of the play's
misogyny. They were also raised earlier in relation to the
ending and Lear's appropriation of Cordelia (p. 98). No
one who discusses the play with women or girls today can be
very confident in asserting that its values are 'timeless'
or 'universal'; teachers find themselves apologising for
Shakespeare's enthusiastic endorsement of what is at last
being widely seen as the unfair and unjustifiable ideology of
patriarchy. As Kathleen McLuskie puts it, 'The misogyny of
King Lear, both the play and its hero, is constructed out of
an ascetic tradition which presents woman as the source of
the primal sin of lust, combining with concerns about the
threat to the family posed by female insubordination' (1985,
p. 106). We may no longer blame Eve for the general
sinfulness of mankind (*Paradise Lost* is another text which is
changing in our classrooms), and we may even wish to
endorse 'female insubordination' – and of a more radical
kind than that of Cordelia, who, like other Shakespearean
heroines (Hermia in *A Midsummer Night's Dream*, Desdemona
in *Othello*) defies her father only in order to assert her duty
to her husband.

We can still find *King Lear* an excellent play in its own
terms, but we must be aware that those terms are no longer
our terms. Since the Second World War awkward questions
have arisen about *The Merchant of Venice*: can this be a great
or classic comedy if it is at the same time racist? Equally
awkward questions are beginning to be raised about other
plays, from *The Taming of the Shrew* to *King Lear*: can these be
great or classic plays if they are at the same time sexist? Does
art, especially 'classic' art, stand somehow outside normal
moral considerations?

Thus the feminist approach turns out to be one way of
denying the 'timelessness' and 'universality' of *King Lear* and
of putting it firmly back into a specific historical context.
This can be done in a perfunctory apologetic way: 'Of course

Shakespeare supported patriarchy; everyone else did at the time and he's really quite enlightened in some ways. . . .' Or it can become part of a larger intellectual project which asks questions about the nature of patriarchy and the possibility of alternative forms of organisation at the levels of both the family and society in general. But the privileged position of the play as some kind of cultural monument which we can only worship has been challenged and the assumption of intrinsic value has shifted.

Feminists are not alone in questioning some of the traditional reasons for ascribing greatness to *King Lear*. Large and rather vague claims about its 'timeless' and 'universal' appeal have in recent years sat rather oddly and inconsistently beside the arguments of Jan Kott, Maynard Mack and others that it has a specific appeal for twentieth-century audiences and readers. We seem to want it to be both at once, apparently because our conception of the greatness of the play depends, as Alan Sinfield puts it, on its being 'capable of speaking positively to all conditions' (Sinfield, 1982, p. 14). But is that conception one which will stand up to examination? Is it even, Sinfield asks, honest? Might we not be guilty of distorting both our own world and the world of the play if we try to force the latter to give us some kind of mirror of the former? Would *King Lear* really lose its cultural authority if we admitted that it was produced under very specific historical and cultural conditions which were different (though not totally different) from those prevailing today? In our anxiety to substantiate Jonson's claim that Shakespeare was 'not of an age but for all time', we may have gone too far in asserting his timelessness and consequently need to restore him to his own age before we can understand in what sense, if any, he is 'our contemporary'. For some people, such an attitude would in itself constitute an attack on the greatness of a play such as *King Lear*, a challenge to its status, an unwelcome limitation of its relevance. For others, it would liberate the play to become more interesting because it would be more specific, more positively itself, and less blandly malleable to changing times and changing critical fashions.

Recent Shakespearean criticism has seen the rise of two slightly different new kinds of historical approach: cultural materialism and new historicism. They are alike in being

interdisciplinary approaches (using the methods not only
of literary critics but also of historians, philosophers,
psychologists, anthropologists, sociologists and so on), and in
rejecting the traditional primacy and isolation of the literary
text. They could also both be seen as deliberate attempts to
escape from the ahistorical and atheoretical perspective of
traditional or 'liberal humanist' criticism. Though similar,
the two approaches do have some significant differences, and
I shall try to outline these below, though I would also refer
the interested reader to Jonathan Dollimore's introductory
essay, 'Shakespeare, Cultural Materialism and the New
Historicism', in *Political Shakespeare* (Dollimore and Sinfield,
1985) and to the essays by Louis Montrose and Jean E.
Howard in the special issue of the journal *English Literary
Renaissance* called 'Studies in Renaissance Historicism' (vol.
16, 1986). There are differences of emphasis and of approach
as well as national differences, since cultural materialism has
developed in Britain and is dominated by British critics,
while new historicism has developed in North America and is
dominated by American critics.

Cultural materialism can be seen as having arisen out of a
body of work done in Britain since the Second World War
which can be broadly described as cultural analysis and
which is associated with a Marxist perspective in general and
with the writings of Raymond Williams in particular. It is
practised by British Shakespearean critics such as Catherine
Belsey, Jonathan Dollimore, John Drakakis, Alan Sinfield
and others whose work appears in *Political Shakespeare*, which
is sub-titled 'New Essays in Cultural Materialism' (Dollimore
and Sinfield, 1985) and in *Alternative Shakespeares* (Drakakis,
1985). These critics aim to relate literary texts to non-literary
phenomena of an economic, social and political nature such
as enclosures and rural poverty, witchcraft, the oppression
of women in the state and the family, class conflict and
challenges to the dominant ideologies (which are themselves
re-examined and restated).

Such work is inevitably concerned with the operations and
relationships of power in society, but it is also concerned
with the broader economic and social perspectives. In
America, new historicism has concentrated much more
specifically on the power of the state and on the interrelation

between that power and various cultural forms. In particular, new historicist critics such as Jonathan Goldberg (1983), Stephen Greenblatt (1980), Louis Montrose (1977, 1980, 1981) and Annabel Patterson (1984) have investigated the points where state power and literature overtly converge in such genres as the court masque and the literary pastoral and in such institutions as patronage and censorship. Both cultural materialists and new historicists have of course wanted to analyse afresh the institution of the theatre itself as a form of representation within a specific context of ideological and political forces.

A major difference between the two approaches, however, is the greater concern of cultural materialists for what is being done with authors such as Shakespeare today. As Louis Montrose puts it, new historicism in America has focused on 'a refiguring of the socio-cultural field in which Renaissance texts were *originally* produced', whereas cultural materialism in Britain has had 'a relatively greater emphasis upon the uses to which the *present* has put its versions of the past' – it has in fact charted 'the history of ideological appropriations of the Renaissance' (1986, p. 7). Cultural materialists, then, are trying not only to recover the Jacobean context of such a work as *King Lear* as fully as possible, but also to examine the ways in which both text and author have been continually *re*-produced in British culture, whether in the theatre or in the classroom, in academic criticism, on television or even in the tourist industry (see also Holderness and McCullough, 1988).

How precisely does all this affect *King Lear* as a canonical or classic text? On one level, both cultural materialism and new historicism *need not* have anything at all to say about the ultimate status or value of particular literary texts. The modes of analysis they employ would be as appropriate to the *Henry VI* plays or to such plays as *Gorboduc* or the earlier *King Leir* as they are to *King Lear* itself, and would not necessarily take them into the realm of making relative value judgements at all. Presumably it is the case that new historicists at least only write about 'great' authors and works because they happen to be readily available – and perhaps out of habit if they have been trained as literary critics. Logically, as Jean E. Howard points out (1986), their work should become not only less centred on 'classic' texts but less literature-based in general, since they assume that 'literature' is an arbitrary designation distinguishing some texts unreasonably from others, and in any case they argue that all texts can only be understood in relation to other representations and practices. This could be seen as a serious displacement amounting, for *King Lear*, to a demotion, if it has to take its place alongside a whole range of other texts – indeed, if it is seen as just one manifestation of the huge 'text' which is Jacobean Britain.

Cultural materialists have more justification for continuing to concentrate on canonical texts, but their reasons for doing so could also seem ominous: in researching and demonstrating the ways in which certain texts and authors have been reproduced or 'appropriated' by subsequent generations, they invite us to see that this is not some mysterious and impersonal process of 'the best' surviving of its own accord but is rather subject to specific historical and cultural circumstances: the greatness of *King Lear* can no longer be seen as a simple natural phenomenon like the greatness of Mount Everest. Different societies and different generations of the same society *make* the play great, sometimes by rewriting it, certainly by rereading it. It was not always perceived as a great play, or even as the greatest of Shakespeare's plays, and there is no guarantee that its current high reputation will continue.

Afterword

IN THE light of the sketch I have given of the history of the evaluation and criticism of *King Lear*, and of the nature of current developments in this field, what can one predict for the future? It would surely be rash to suppose that now at last in the late twentieth century we have finally recognised the true qualities of the play and have elevated it to a permanent and unassailable position. History seems rather to indicate that such a stasis is difficult if not impossible to achieve: if *King Lear* continues to be reread, it will continue to be reinterpreted, both in performance and on the page. In some sense all future readings could be said to be already 'there' in the text, but we have to wait for the historical circumstances which will make them visible.

There is in any event a considerable degree of certainty that *King Lear* will be reread for some time to come. It seems unlikely that we shall soon find ourselves again in the somewhat precarious position of the eighteenth century, when Shakespeare's original version was not performed at all and was read only by a tine elite. The present power of educational institutions and more widespread access to them should at least prevent that from happening. We might find ourselves faced with almost the opposite danger: the academic community (not to mention the Royal Shakespeare Company) having so much invested in a particular canon of texts that it is reluctant to permit any change. But may not the institutions themselves be under pressure to work upon the play in ways which challenge traditional attitudes and reopen the debates? To take the greatness of *King Lear* for granted would be to deaden the desire to explore and question the text at every level.

References

Alpers, Paul J., 'King Lear and the Theory of the "Sight Pattern"', in Reuben A. Brower and Richard Poirier (eds), In Defence of Reading (New York, 1962) pp. 133–52.

Barber, C. L., 'The Family in Shakespeare's Development: Tragedy and Sacredness', in Murray M. Schwartz and Coppélia Kahn (eds), Representing Shakespeare (Baltimore and London, 1980) pp. 188–202.

Battenhouse, Roy W., Shakespearean Tragedy: Its Art and Its Christian Premises (Bloomington, Ind., and London, 1969).

Bennett, Josephine Waters, 'The Storm Within: the Madness of Lear', Shakespeare Quarterly, 13 (1962) 137–55.

Bethell, S. L., Shakespeare and the Popular Dramatic Tradition (London, 1944).

Black, James, 'King Lear: Art Upside-Down', Shakespeare Survey, 33 (1980) 35–42.

Blau, Herbert, 'A Subtext Based on Nothing', Tulane Drama Review, 8(1963) 122–32.

Blayney, Peter W. M., The Texts of 'King Lear' and Their Origins (Cambridge, 1982).

Booth, Stephen, 'King Lear', 'Macbeth', Indefinition, and Tragedy (New Haven, Conn., and London, 1983).

Bradley, A. C., Shakespearean Tragedy (London, 1904); excerpted in Kermode (1969) pp. 83–117 and in Muir (1984) pp. 31–54.

Brooke, Nicholas, 'The Ending of King Lear', in Edward A. Bloom (ed.), Shakespeare 1564–1964 (Providence, RI, 1964) pp. 71–87; excerpted in Muir (1984) pp. 219–21.

Bullough, Geoffrey, Narrative and Dramatic Sources of Shakespeare, VII (London and New York, 1973).

Campbell, Oscar James, 'The Salvation of Lear', English Literary History, 15 (1948) 93–109.

Cavell, Stanley, Must We Mean What We Say? (New York, 1969).

Champion, Larry S., 'King Lear': An Annotated Bibliography, 2 vols (New York and London, 1980).

Clemen, Wolfgang, *The Development of Shakespeare's Imagery* (London, 1951).

Colie, Rosalie L., *Paradoxia Epidemica* (Princeton, NJ, 1966).

——, 'Reason and Need: *King Lear* and the "Crisis" of the Aristocracy' (1974a), in Colie and Flahiff (1974) pp. 185–219.

——, 'The Energies of Endurance: Biblical Echo in *King Lear*' (1974b), in Colie and Flahiff (1974) pp. 117–44.

Colie, Rosalie L., and Flahiff, F. T. (eds), *Some Facets of 'King Lear': Essays in Prismatic Criticism* (Toronto and London, 1974).

Crosby, Ernest, *Shakespeare and the Working Classes* (London, 1903).

Danby, John F., *Shakespeare's Doctrine of Nature: A Study of 'King Lear'* (London, 1949).

——, *Poets on Fortune's Hill* (London, 1952).

Danson, Lawrence (ed.), *On 'King Lear'* (Princeton, NJ, 1981).

Davison, Peter, *Contemporary Drama and the Popular Dramatic Tradition in England* (London, 1982).

Delany, Paul, '*King Lear* and the Decline of Feudalism', *PMLA*, 92 (1977) 430–1.

Dollimore, Jonathan, *Radical Tragedy* (Brighton, 1984).

——, 'Shakespeare, Cultural Materialism and the New Historicism', in Dollimore and Sinfield (1985) pp. 2–17.

Dollimore, Jonathan, and Sinfield, Alan (eds), *Political Shakespeare* (Manchester, 1985).

Doran, Madeleine, ' "Give me the map there." Command, Question and Assertion in *King Lear*', in *Shakespeare's Dramatic Language* (Madison, Wis., 1976) pp. 92–119.

Drakakis, John (ed.), *Alternative Shakespeares* (London and New York, 1985).

Driscoll, James P., 'The Vision of *King Lear*', *Shakespeare Studies*, 10 (1977) 159–89.

Dundes, Alan, ' "To love my father all": A Psychoanalytic Study of the Folktale Source of *King Lear*', *Interpreting Folklore* (Bloomington, Ind., 1980).

Duthie, G. I. (ed.), *King Lear*, Cambridge Shakespeare edn (Cambridge, 1960).

Edwards, Philip, *Shakespeare and the Confines of Art* (London, 1968).

Eliot, T. S., *What is a Classic?* (London, 1945).

Elton, William R., *'King Lear' and the Gods* (San Marino, Calif., 1966); excerpted in Kermode (1969) pp. 245–64.

Empson, William, *Some Versions of Pastoral* (London, 1935).

——, *The Structure of Complex Words* (London, 1951).

——, 'Next Time, a Wheel of Fire', *Essays in Criticism*, 17 (1967) 95–102.

Erickson, Peter, *Patriarchal Structures in Shakespeare's Drama* (Berkeley, Calif., Los Angeles and London, 1985).

Evans, Bertrand, *Shakespeare's Tragic Practice* (Oxford, 1979).

Everett, Barbara, 'The New *King Lear*', *Critical Quarterly*, 2 (1960) 325–39; reprinted in Kermode (1969) pp. 184–202.

Fiedler, Leslie A., and Baker, Houston A., *Opening Up the Canon* (Baltimore and London, 1981).

Flahiff, F. T., 'Edgar: Once and Future King', in Colie and Flahiff (1974) pp. 221–37.

Fleissner, Robert F., 'The "Nothing" Element in *King Lear*', *Shakespeare Quarterly*, 13 (1962) 67–70.

Foakes, R. A., 'Suggestions for a New Approach to Shakespeare's Imagery', *Shakespeare Survey*, 5 (1982) 81–92.

Fowler, Alastair, 'Genre and the Literary Canon', *New Literary History*, 11 (1979) 97–119.

French, A. L., *Shakespeare and the Critics* (Cambridge, 1972).

Freud, Sigmund, 'The Theme of the Three Caskets' (1913) in *Collected Papers* (London, 1924–5); excerpted in Muir (1984) p. 57.

Goldberg, Jonathan, *James I and the Politics of Literature* (Baltimore and London, 1983).

Goldberg, S. L., *An Essay on 'King Lear'* (Cambridge, 1974).

Goldman, Michael, '*King Lear*: Acting and Feeling', in Danson (1981) 25–46.

Granville-Barker, Harley, *Prefaces to Shakespeare* (London, 1946); excerpted in Muir (1984) pp. 59–82.

Greenblatt, Stephen, *Renaissance Self-Fashioning* (Chicago and London, 1980).

——, 'Shakespeare and the Exorcists', in Patricia Parker and Geoffrey Hartman (eds), *Shakespeare and the Question of Theory* (New York and London, 1985) pp. 163–87.

Greenfield, Thomas A., 'Excellent Things in Women: The Emergence of Cordelia', *South Atlantic Bulletin*, 42 (1977) 44–52.

Harbage, Alfred, *Conceptions of Shakespeare* (Cambridge, Mass., 1966).

Hawkes, Terence, '"Love" in *King Lear*', *Review of English Studies*, 10 (1959) 178–81; reprinted in Kermode (1969) pp. 179–83.

Heilman, Robert B., *This Great Stage: Image and Structure in 'King Lear'* (Baton Rouge, LA, 1948).

Hibbard, G. R., 'King Lear: A Retrospect, 1939–79', Shakespeare Survey, 33 (1980) 1–12.

Hoeniger, F. D., 'The Artist Exploring the Primitive: King Lear', in Colie and Flahiff (1974) pp. 89–102.

Holderness, Graham, and McCullough, Christopher (eds) The Shakespeare Myth (Manchester, 1988).

Holland, Norman N., 'How Can Dr Johnson's Remarks on Cordelia's Death Add to My Own Response?', in Geoffrey H. Hartman (ed.), Psychoanalysis and the Question of the Text (Baltimore and London, 1978) pp. 18–44.

Holloway, John, The Story of the Night (London, 1961); excerpted in Kermode (1969) pp. 203–27.

Honigmann, E. A. J., Shakespeare: Seven Tragedies (London, 1976).

——, Shakespeare: The 'Lost Years' (Manchester, 1985).

Howard, Jean E., 'The New Historicism in Renaissance Studies', English Literary Renaissance, 16 (1986) 13–43.

Hunter, G. K. (ed.), King Lear, New Penguin Shakespeare edn (Harmondsworth, 1972).

Hunter, R. G., Shakespeare and the Mystery of God's Judgements (Athens, Ga., 1976).

Isenberg, Arnold, 'Cordelia Absent', Shakespeare Quarterly, 2 (1951) 185–94.

Johnson, Samuel, The Plays of William Shakespeare (London, 1765); excerpted in Kermode (1969) pp. 27–30 and Muir (1984) pp. 1–3.

Jones, Emrys, Scenic Form in Shakespeare (Oxford, 1971).

Jones, James H., 'Leir and Lear: Matthew 5.33–7, The Turning Point, and the Rescue Theme', Comparative Drama, 4 (1970–1) 125–61.

Jorgensen, Paul A., Lear's Self-Discovery (Berkeley, Calif. and Los Angeles, 1967).

Keast, W. R., 'Imagery and Meaning in the Interpretation of King Lear', Modern Philology, 47 (1949) 45–64.

Kermode, Frank, 'Survival of the Classic', in Shakespeare, Spenser, Donne (London, 1971) pp. 164–80.

——, The Classic (London, 1975).

——, 'Institutional Control of Interpretation', Salmagundi, 43 (1979) 72–86.

Kermode, Frank (ed.), Shakespeare: 'King Lear': A Casebook (London, 1969).

Kernan, Alvin B., 'King Lear and the Shakespearean Pageant of History', in Danson (1981) pp. 7–24.

Kerrigan, John, 'Revision, Adaptation and the Fool in *King Lear*', in Taylor and Warren (1983) pp. 195–245.

Kirschbaum, Leo, *The True Text of 'King Lear'* (Baltimore, 1945).

———, 'Albany', *Shakespeare Survey*, 13 (1960) 20–9.

Knight, G. Wilson, *The Wheel of Fire* (London, 1930); excerpted in Kermode (1969) pp. 118–36 and Muir (1984) pp. 83–101.

———, *Tolstoy's Attack on Shakespeare*, English Association pamphlet (London, 1934); repr. in Knight, *The Wheel of Fire*, rev. edn (London, 1949).

Knights, L. C., 'On Historical Scholarship and the Interpretation of Shakespeare', *Sewanee Review*, 63 (1955) 223–40.

———, *Some Shakespearean Themes* (London, 1959).

Kott, Jan, *Shakespeare Our Contemporary* (London, 1965); excerpted in Kermode (1969) pp. 270–92.

Kozintsev, Grigori, *'King Lear': The Space of Tragedy* (London, 1977).

Krieger, Elliot, 'Social Relations and Social Order in *Much Ado About Nothing*', *Shakespeare Survey*, 32 (1979) 49–61.

Lamb, Charles, 'On the Tragedies of Shakespeare', *The Reflector*, 4 (London, 1812); excerpted in Kermode (1969) pp. 44–5 and Muir (1984) pp. 5–6.

Lascelles, Mary, *'King Lear* and Doomsday', *Shakespeare Survey*, 26 (1973) 69–79.

Levin, Harry, 'The Heights and the Depths: A Scene from *King Lear*', in John Garrett (ed.), *More Talking of Shakespeare* (London, 1959) pp. 87–103; reprinted in Muir (1984) pp. 145–63.

Levin, Richard, *The Multiple Plot in English Renaissance Drama* (Chicago and London, 1971).

———, *New Readings vs. Old Plays* (Chicago and London, 1979).

Lindheim, Nancy R., *'King Lear* as Pastoral Tragedy', in Colie and Flahiff (1974) pp. 169–84.

Lipking, Lawrence, 'Aristotle's Sister: A Poetics of Abandonment', *Critical Inquiry*, 10 (1983) 61–81.

Long, Michael, *The Unnatural Scene* (London, 1976).

Mack, Maynard, *'King Lear' in Our Time* (Berkeley, Calif., and Los Angeles, 1965); excerpted in Kermode (1969) pp. 51–82 and Muir (1984) pp. 223–49.

Marks, Carol L., '"Speak what we feel": The End of *King Lear*', *English Language Notes*, 5 (1968) 163–71.

Marowitz, Charles, 'Lear Log', *Tulane Drama Review*, 8 (1963) 103–21.

Mason, H. A., *Shakespeare's Tragedies of Love* (London, 1970).

McCombie, Frank, 'Medium and Message in *As You Like It* and *King Lear*', *Shakespeare Survey*, 33 (1980) 67–80.

McLuhan, Marshall, *The Gutenberg Galaxy* (Toronto and London, 1962).

McLuskie, Kathleen, 'The Patriarchal Bard: Feminist Criticism and Shakespeare: *King Lear* and *Measure for Measure*', in Dollimore and Sinfield (1985) pp. 88–108.

McNeir, Waldo, 'Cordelia's Return in *King Lear*', *English Language Notes*, 6 (1969) 172–6.

Melchiori, Barbara, 'Still Harping on my Daughter', *English Miscellany*, 11 (1960) 59–74.

Miller, Ronald F., '*King Lear* and the Comic Form', *Genre*, 8 (1975) 1–25.

Montrose, Louis, 'Celebration and Insinuation: Sir Philip Sidney and the Motives of Elizabethan Courtship', *Renaissance Drama*, 8 (1977) 3–35.

——, ' "Eliza, Queene of shepheardes" and the Pastoral of Power', *English Literary Renaissance*, 10 (1980) 153–82.

——, ' "The Place of a Brother" in *As You Like It*: Social Process and Comic Form', *Shakespeare Quarterly*, 32 (1981) 28–54.

——, 'Renaissance Literary Studies and the Subject of History', *English Literary Renaissance*, 16 (1986) 5–12.

Morris, Ivor, 'Cordelia and Lear', *Shakespeare Quarterly*, 8 (1957) 141–58.

Moulton, Richard G., *Shakespeare as a Dramatic Artist* (Oxford, 1885).

Muir, Kenneth, 'Madness in *King Lear*', *Shakespeare Survey*, 13 (1960) 30–40.

——, 'Shakespeare's Imagery: Then and Now', *Shakespeare Survey*, 18 (1965) 46–57.

Muir, Kenneth (ed.), *King Lear*, New Arden Shakespeare edn (London, 1952).

——, '*King Lear: Critical Essays* (New York and London, 1984).

Murphy, John L., *Darkness and Devils* (Athens, Ohio, and London, 1984).

Murry, John Middleton, 'The Paradox of *King Lear*', *Shakespeare* (London, 1936).

Nevo, Ruth, *Tragic Form in Shakespeare* (Princeton, NJ, 1972).

Novy, Marianne L., *Love's Argument: Gender Relations in Shakespeare* (Chapel Hill, NC, and London, 1984).

Nowottny, Winifred, 'Lear's Questions', *Shakespeare Survey*, 10 (1957) 90–7.

——, 'Some Aspects of the Style of *King Lear*', *Shakespeare Survey*, 13 (1960) 49–57.

Oates, Joyce Carol, '"Is this the promised end?": The Tragedy of *King Lear*', *Contraries* (New York, 1981) pp. 51–81.

Orgel, Stephen, 'Shakespeare and the Kinds of Drama', *Critical Inquiry*, 6 (1980) 107–23.

Orwell, George, 'Lear, Tolstoy and the Fool', *Shooting an Elephant* (London, 1947); reprinted in Kermode (1969) pp. 150–68 and Muir (1984) pp. 119–36.

Parker, Patricia, and Hartman, Geoffrey (eds), *Shakespeare and the Question of Theory* (New York and London, 1985).

Patterson, Annabel, *Censorship and Interpretation* (Madison, Wis., 1984).

Peat, Derek, '"And that's true too": *King Lear* and the Tension of Uncertainty', *Shakespeare Survey*, 33 (1980) 43–53.

Raison, Bertrand, and Toubiana, Serge, *Le livre de 'Ran'* (Paris, 1985).

Reibetanz, John, *The Lear World: A Study of 'King Lear' in its Dramatic Context* (Toronto and London, 1977).

Roche, Thomas P., '"Nothing almost sees miracles": Tragic Knowledge in *King Lear*', in Danson (1981) pp. 136–62.

Rosenberg, John D., 'King Lear and his Comforters', *Essays in Criticism*, 16 (1966) 135–46.

Rosenberg, Marvin, *The Masks of 'King Lear'* (Berkeley, Calif., Los Angeles and London, 1972).

Sahel, Pierre, '*King Lear*: A War of the Theatres', *Aligarh Journal of English Studies*, 8 (1983) 186–204.

Salgado, Gamini, '*King Lear: Text and Performance* (Basingstoke and London, 1984).

Schoff, Francis G., 'King Lear: Moral Example or Tragic Protagonist', *Shakespeare Quarterly*, 13 (1962) 157–72.

Schwartz, Murray M., and Kahn, Coppélia (eds), *Representing Shakespeare* (Baltimore and London, 1980).

Serpieri, Alessandro, 'The Breakdown of Medieval Hierarchy in *King Lear*', in Seymour Chatman, Umberto Eco and Jean-Marie Klinkenberg (eds), *A Semiotic Landscape* (The Hague, 1979) pp. 1067–72.

Shaw, John, '*King Lear*: The Final Lines', *Essays in Criticism*, 16 (1966) 261–7.

Sinfield, Alan, '*King Lear* versus *Lear* at Stratford', *Critical Quarterly*, 24 (1982) 5–14.

——, 'Shakespeare and Education', in Dollimore and Sinfield (1985) pp. 134–57.

Sisson, C. J., *Shakespeare's Tragic Justice* (London, 1962); excerpted in Kermode (1969) pp. 228–44.

Smith, Barbara Herrnstein, 'Contingencies of Value', *Critical Inquiry*, 10 (1983) 1–35.

Snyder, Susan, *The Comic Matrix of Shakespeare's Tragedies* (Princeton, NJ, 1979).

——, '*King Lear* and the Psychology of Dying', *Shakespeare Quarterly*, 33 (1982) 449–60.

Speaight, Robert, 'Shakespeare in Britain', *Shakespeare Quarterly*, 4 (1963) 419–21; reprinted in Muir (1984) pp. 275–9.

Spurgeon, Caroline F. E., *Shakespeare's Imagery* (Cambridge, 1935).

Stampfer, J., 'The Catharsis of *King Lear*', *Shakespeare Survey*, 13 (1960) 1–10; reprinted in Muir (1984) pp. 203–17.

Stone, Lawrence, *The Crisis of the Aristocracy, 1558–1641* (Oxford, 1965).

——, *The Family, Sex and Marriage in England, 1500–1800* (London, 1977).

Stone, P. W. K., *The Textual History of 'King Lear'* (London, 1980).

Styan, J. L., *The Shakespeare Revolution* (Cambridge, 1977).

Taylor, Gary, 'Revolutions of Perspective: *King Lear*', in *Moment by Moment by Shakespeare* (London, 1985).

Taylor, Gary, and Warren, Michael (eds), *The Division of the Kingdoms* (Oxford, 1983).

Thompson, Ann, 'Who Sees Double in the Double Plot? in Malcolm Bradbury and David Palmer (eds), *Shakespearian Tragedy* (1984) pp. 47–75.

Thompson, Ann and John O., *Shakespeare, Meaning and Metaphor* (Brighton, 1987).

Thomson, P. W., 'King Lear and the Actors', *Aligarh Journal of English Studies*, 8 (1983) 167–79.

Tillyard, E. M. W., *The Elizabethan World Picture* (London, 1943).

Tolstoy, Leo, 'Shakespeare and the Drama', preface to Ernest Crosby, *Shakespeare and the Working Classes* (London, 1903).

Urkowitz, Steven, *Shakespeare's Revision of 'King Lear'* (Princeton, NJ, 1980).

Walton, J. K., 'Lear's Last Speech', *Shakespeare Survey*, 13 (1960) 11–19.

Warren, Michael J., 'Quarto and Folio *King Lear* and the Interpretation of Albany and Edgar', in David Bevington and Jay L. Halio (eds), *Shakespeare, Pattern of Excelling Nature* (Newark, Del., 1978) pp. 95–107.

——, 'The Diminution of Kent', in Taylor and Warren (1983) pp. 59–73.

Webster, Margaret, *Shakespeare Today* (London, 1957).

Weimann, Robert, 'Shakespeare and the Study of Metaphor', *New Literary History*, 6 (1974) 149–67.

Weiss, Theodore, 'As the Wind Sits: The Poetics of *King Lear*', in Danson (1981) pp. 61–90.

Welsford, Enid, *The Fool* (London, 1935); excerpted in Kermode (1969) pp. 137–49 and Muir (1984) pp. 103–18.

Wickham, Glynne, 'From Tragedy to Tragi-comedy: *King Lear* as Prologue', *Shakespeare Survey*, 26 (1973) 33–48.

Widdowson, Peter (ed.), *Re-Reading English* (London, 1982).

Wittreich, Joseph, *'Image of that Horror': History, Prophecy, and Apocalypse in 'King Lear'* (San Marino, Calif., 1984).

Young, David, *The Heart's Forest: A Study of Shakespeare's Pastoral Plays* (New Haven, Conn., and London, 1972).

Index

Alpers, Paul J., 52–3
Annesley, Brian, 22–3
Antony and Cleopatra, 33
Aristotle, 33
As You Like It, 19, 54

Bacon, Francis, 25
Baker, Houston A., 64
Barber, C. L., 15
Battenhouse, Roy W., 35
Beckett, Samuel, 21, 47–9, 50
Belsey, Catherine, 78
Bennett, Josephine Waters, 56
Bethell, S. L., 41
Birth of Merlin, 22
Black, James, 56
Blau, Herbert, 46
Blayney, Peter W. M., 12
Bond, Edward, 48, 50
Booth, Stephen, 42
Bradley, A. C., 15–16, 31, 36, 40–3, 45, 56, 68
Brecht, Bertolt, 47–9
Brook, Peter, 45–50
Brooke, Nicholas, 39
Bullough, Geoffrey, 23

Campbell, Oscar James, 18, 34, 37
Cavell, Stanley, 58, 72
Champion, Larry S., 9, 53
Chapman, George, 18
Clemen, Wolfgang, 52
Coleridge, Samuel, 74
Colie, Rosalie L., 26–9, 34, 53
Congreve, William, 62
Coriolanus, 71
Crosby, Ernest, 69
Cymbeline, 19

Danby, John F., 19, 24–5, 28, 37, 39
Daniel, Samuel, 23
Darwin, Charles, 68
Davison, Peter, 41
Dekker, Thomas, 23
Delany, Paul, 26
Dollimore, Jonathan, 29, 31–2, 78
Doran, Madeleine, 54
Drakakis, John, 78
Driscoll, James P., 37, 57
Dundes, Alan, 15, 57
Dürrenmatt, Friedrich, 21, 47
Duthie, G. I., 41

Edwards, Philip, 19
Eisenstein, Sergei M., 50
Eliot, T. S., 61–2
Elizabeth, I., 22–3
Elliot, Michael, 51
Elton, William R., 17, 24, 35
Empson, William, 16, 36, 54, 57
Erickson, Peter, 58
Evans, Bertrand, 16
Everett, Barbara, 31, 38

Fiedler, Leslie A., 64
Flahiff, F. T., 24
Fleissner, Robert F., 36
Fletcher, John, 18
Florio, John, 14
Foakes, R. A., 53
Fowler, Alastair, 63
French, A. L., 17, 31, 38–9, 72–3
Freud, Sigmund, 57, 72

Goldberg, Jonathan, 29, 79
Goldberg, S. L., 41

Goldman, Michael, 46
Gorboduc, 22–3
Granville-Barker, Harley, 43, 45
Greenblatt, Stephen, 29–30, 79
Greenfield, Thomas A., 57

Hamlet, 13, 33, 35, 49, 68, 71
Harbage, Alfred, 67, 74
Harsnett, Samuel, 14, 29–30, 34
Hawkes, Terence, 54
Hazlitt, William, 44, 68
Heilman, Robert B., 52–3
Henry V, 66
Henry VI, 54
Hibbard, G. R., 31
Higgins, John, 14
Hobbes, Thomas, 25
Hoeniger, F. D., 15
Holderness, Graham, 79
Holinshed, Raphael, 13–14
Holland, Norman N., 39
Holloway, John, 23, 37
Homer, 61
Honigmann, E. A. J., 32, 56
Hooker, Richard, 25
Hordern, Michael, 51
Howard, Jean E., 78–80
Hume, David, 61
Hunter, G. K., 41, 43
Hunter, R. G., 35

Ionesco, Eugene, 21
Isenberg, Arnold, 57

James I, 13
James II, 27
Johnson, Samuel, 30, 39
Jones, Emrys, 16–19, 34, 42, 54
Jones, James H., 34
Jonson, Ben, 67, 77
Jorgensen, Paul A., 24, 38
Julius Caesar, 33

Kean, Charles, 44
Kean, Edmund, 44
Keast, W. R., 52–3
Keats, John, 68
Kermode, Frank, 58, 62, 65, 69–71
Kernan, Alvin B., 28

Kerrigan, John, 57
King John, 33–4, 54
King Lear, 13–15, 19, 22, 34, 68
Kirschbaum, Leo, 57
Knight, G. Wilson, 21, 37, 39, 69
Knights, L. C., 24, 28, 39, 61–2
Kott, Jan, 21, 37, 45, 47, 50, 77
Kozintsev, Grigori, 45, 49–50
Krieger, Elliot, 69
Kurosawa, Akira, 45, 50
Kyd, Thomas, 67
Kyle, Barry, 48

Lamb, Charles, 42–4, 67
Lascelles, Mary, 23
Lawrence, D. H., 72
Levin, Harry, 55
Levin, Richard, 17, 74–5
Lindheim, Nancy R., 19
Lipking, Lawrence, 66
Locrine, 22–3
Long, Michael, 20, 41

Macbeth, 35, 50
Mack, Maynard, 20, 23, 36, 40, 44, 46–9, 77
Macready, William C., 44
Marks, Carol L., 42
Marowitz, Charles, 47–8
Marston, John, 18
Mason, H. A., 17, 39, 41–2, 72
McCombie, Frank, 19
McCullough, Christopher, 79
McLuhan, Marshall, 25
McLuskie, Kathleen, 58, 76
McNeir, Waldo, 41
Measure for Measure, 74
Melchiori, Barbara, 15, 57
Merchant of Venice, 76
Merry Wives of Windsor, 43
Middleton, Thomas, 18
Midsummer Night's Dream, 76
Miller, Jonathan, 51
Miller, Ronald F., 20
Millett, Kate, 66
Milton, John, 66, 76
Misfortunes of Arthur, 22
Montaigne, M. de., 14
Montrose, Louis, 78–9

Morris, Ivor, 36
Moulton, Richard G., 16
Muir, Kenneth, 13, 34, 39, 51, 53, 55–6, 71
Munday, Anthony, 23
Murphy, John L., 30
Murry, John Middleton, 71

Nevo, Ruth, 16, 37, 40
Noble, Adrian, 48
Novy, Marianne L., 58
Nowottny, Winifred, 53–4

Oates, Joyce Carol, 71–2
Olivier, Laurence, 51
Orgel, Stephen, 20
Orwell, George, 16, 69–71
Othello, 13, 33–5, 68, 71, 76

Patterson, Annabel, 79
Peat, Derek, 40–1
Pericles, 15, 19, 43

Raison, Bertrand, 50
Ran, 50
Rape of Lucrece, 63
Reibetanz, John, 18, 41
Richard III, 35
Roche, Thomas P., 38
Rosenberg, John D., 41
Rosenberg, Marvin, 45, 54–5

Sahel, Pierre, 46
Salgado, Gamini, 47
Schoff, Francis G., 28
Serpieri, Alessandro, 26, 54
Shaw, George Bernard, 69
Shaw, John, 41
Sidney, Philip, 14, 19
Sinfield, Alan, 48–9, 64, 77–8
Sisson, C. J., 23, 56
Smith, Barbara Herrnstein, 61, 64–5

Snyder, Susan, 18, 20, 40, 42
Speaight, Robert, 48–9
Spenser, Edmund, 14
Spurgeon, Caroline F. E., 52
Stampfer, J., 39
Stone, Lawrence, 26–9
Stone, P. W. K., 12
Styan, J. L., 47

Taming of the Shrew, 66, 76
Tate, Nahum, 27, 43–4, 48, 67, 70
Taylor, Gary, 12, 55
Tempest, 15, 19
Thompson, Ann, 16
Thompson, Ann and John O., 53
Thomson, P. W., 46
Throne of Blood, 50
Tillyard, E. M. W., 28–9
Timon of Athens, 71
Titus Andronicus, 67
Tolstoy, Leo, 16, 37, 68–71
Toubiana, Serge, 50
Troilus and Cressida, 33

Urkowitz, Steven, 12, 57

Venus and Adonis, 63
Virgil, 61–2

Walton, J. K., 40
Warren, Michael J., 12, 57
Webster, Margaret, 16, 42–3
Weimann, Robert, 53
Weiss, Theodore, 56
Welsford, Enid, 57
Wickham, Glynne, 19, 23
Widdowson, Peter, 65
Williams, Raymond, 78
Winter's Tale, 15, 19
Wittreich, Joseph, 23

Young, David, 20